D0923371

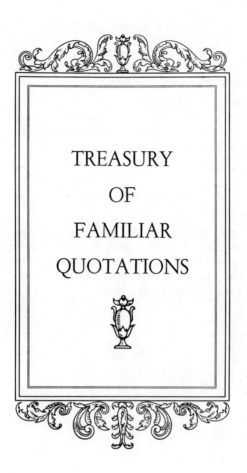

TREASURY
OF
FAMILIAR
QUOTATIONS

AVENEL BOOKS
A DIVISION OF CROWN PUBLISHERS, INC.
NEW YORK

PREFACE

A successful writer or speaker wisely and freely falls back on the good things that have been written or said by others.

Users of these quotations are as wise as if they had originated them; for they could never originate even one-tenth of the material that they can borrow.

As you turn these pages, you will be reminded of many wise and witty sayings you have forgotten and discover others you never knew existed.

These quotations are the cream of the great writings of world literature. We hope that you enjoy this book enough to make you want to read, in their entirety, the lines from which these quotations are taken.

517117746
Copyright © MCMLV, MCMLXIII by Ottenheimer Publishers, Inc.
All rights reserved.
This edition is published by Avenel Books
a division of Crown Publishers, Inc.
by arrangement with Ottenheimer Publishers, Inc.
Manufactured in the United States Of America
Formerly titled: Book of Familiar Quotations

ABILITY.

Ability wins us the esteem of the true men; luck that of the people.   *La Rochefoucauld.*

Consider well what your strength is equal to, and what exceeds your ability.   *Horace.*

An able man shows his spirit by gentle words and resolute actions; he is neither hot nor timid.   *Chesterfield.*

ABSENCE.

In my Lucia's absence
Life hangs upon me, and becomes a burden;
I am ten times undone, while hope, and fear,
And grief, and rage and love rise up at once,
And with variety of pain distract me.   *Addison.*

O thou who dost inhabit in my breast,
Leave not the mansion, so long tenantless;
Lest growing ruinous the building fall,
And leave no memory of what it was.   *Shakespeare.*

ABSTINENCE.

To set the mind above the appetites is the end of abstinence, which one of the Fathers observes to be, not a *virtue*, but the *groundwork of a virtue*.   *Johnson.*

ABUSE.

The bitter clamour of two eager tongues.   *Shakespeare.*

ACCOUNT.

No reckoning made, but sent to my account
With all my imperfections on my head.   *Shakespeare.*

ACQUAINTANCE.

There is a wide difference between general acquaintance

1

and companionship. You may salute a man and exchange compliments with him daily, yet know nothing of his character, his inmost tastes and feelings. *Wm. Matthews.*

ACQUAINTANCES.

If a man does not make new acquaintances, as he advances through life, he will soon find himself left alone. A man should keep his friendship in constant repair. *Johnson.*

Make the most of the day, by determining to spend it on *two* sorts of acquaintances only—those by whom something may be got, and those from whom something may be learned. *Colton.*

ACQUIREMENTS.

That which we acquire with the most difficulty we retain the longest; as those who have earned a fortune are usually more careful of it than those who have inherited one. *Colton.*

ACTING.

All the world's a stage. *Shakespeare.*

ACTION.

We should often be ashamed of our very best actions, if the world only saw the motives which caused them.
La Rochefoucauld.

When we cannot act as we wish, we must act as we can.
Terrence.

The end of man is an action, and not a thought, though it were the noblest. *Carlyle.*

Think that day lost whose low descending sun
Views from thy hand no noble action done. *Jacob Bobart.*

Advise well before you begin, and when you have maturely considered, then act with promptitude. *Sallust.*

Strong reasons make strong actions.   *Shakespeare.*

ACTIONS.

Our actions are our own; their consequences belong to Heaven.   *Francis.*

The evil that men do lives after them;
The good is oft interr'd with their bones.   *Shakespeare.*

All our actions take
Their hues from the complexion of the heart,
As landscapes their variety from light.   *W. T. Bacon.*

Actions of the last age are like almanacs of the last year.
        Sir Thomas Denham.

Act well at the moment, and you have performed a good action to all eternity.   *Lavater.*

ACTIVITY.

Run, if you like, but try to keep your breath;
Work like a man, but don't be worked to death.   *Holmes.*

ACTS.

The best portion of a good man's life,
His little, nameless, unremembered acts of kindness and
   of love.   *Wordsworth.*

Our acts our angels are, or good or ill,
Our fatal shadows that walk by us still.   *John Fletcher.*

ACUTENESS.

The keen spirit
Seizes the prompt occasion—makes the thought
Start into instant action, and at once
Plans and performs, resolves and executes.   *Hannah Moore.*

A man who knows the world will not only make the most

of everything he does know, but of many things that he does not know; and will gain more credit by his adroit mode of hiding his ignorance than the pedant by his awkward attempt to exhibit his erudition. *Colton.*

ADVERSITY.

Adversity borrows its sharpest sting from our impatience.
Bishop Horne.

Adversity has the effect of eliciting talents, which in prosperous circumstances would have lain dormant. *Horace.*

The good are better made by ill,
As odors crush'd are sweeter still. *Rogers.*

The firmest friendships have been formed in mutual adversity, as iron is most strongly welded by the fiercest fire.

Such a house broke!
So noble a master fallen! All gone and not
One friend to take his fortune by the arm
And go along with him. *Shakespeare.*

Adversity's sweet milk, Philosophy. *Shakespeare.*

He is the most wretched of men who has never felt adversity.

Sweet are the uses of adversity,
Which like the toad, ugly and venomous,
Wears yet a precious jewel in his head;
And this our life, exempt from public haunt,
Find tongues in trees, books in the running brooks,
Sermons in stones, and good in everything. *Shakespeare.*

We ask advice, but we mean approbation. *Colton.*

Let no man presume to give advice to others that has not first given good counsel to himself. *Seneca.*

Love all, trust a few.
Do wrong to none; be able for thine enemy
Rather in power than use; and keep thy friend
Under thine own life's key; be checked for silence,
But never taxed for speech. *Shakespeare.*

The worst men often give the best advice.   *Bailey.*

We give advice, but we cannot give the wisdom to profit
by it.   *La Rochefoucauld.*

Give thy thoughts no tongue,
Nor any unproportioned thought his act.
Be thou familiar, but by no means vulgar.
The friends thou hast, and their adoption tried,
Grapple them to thy soul with hooks of steel;
But do not dull thy palm with entertainment
Of each new-hatched, unfledged comrade.
Beware
Of entrance to a quarrel; but, being in,
Bear it that the opposer may beware of thee.
Give every man thine ear, but few thy voice.
Take each man's censure, but reserve thy judgment.
Costly thy habit as thy purse can buy,
But not expressed in fancy; rich, not gaudy;
For the apparel oft proclaims the man.
Neither a borrower nor a lender be,
For loan oft loses both itself and friend;
And borrowing dulls the edge of husbandry.
This above all: To thine own self be true;
And it must follow, as the night the day,
Thou cans't not then be false to any man.   *Shakespeare.*

He who can take advice is sometimes superior to him who
can give it.   *Von Knebel.*

Let no man value at a little price
A virtuous woman's counsel; her winged spirit
Is feathered often times with heavenly words,
And, like her beauty, ravishing and pure.   *Chapman.*

AFFECTION.

Fathers alone a father's heart can know
What secret tides of still enjoyment flow
When brothers love, but if their hate succeeds,
They wage the war, but 'tis the father bleeds.   *Young.*

AFFECTIONS.

Of all the tyrants the world affords,
Our own affections are the fiercest lords. *Earl of Sterling.*

O you much partial gods!
Why gave ye men affections, and not power
To govern them? *Ludovick Barry.*

Nothing can occur beyond the strength of faith to sustain,
or, transcending the resources of religion, to relieve. *Binney.*
Man is born to trouble, as the sparks fly upward. *Job* v.7.

AGE.

Age sits with decent grace upon his visage,
And worthily becomes his silver locks;
He bears the marks of many years well spent,
Of virtue truth well tried, and wise experience. *Rowe.*

As you are old and reverend, you should be wise.
Shakespeare.

These are the effects of doting age,
Vain doubts, and idle cares, and over caution. *Dryden.*

But an old age serene and bright,
And lovely as a Lapland night,
Shall lead thee to thy grave. *Wordsworth.*

How blest is he who crowns, in shades like these,
A youth of labor with an age of ease. *Goldsmith.*

Eternal sunshine settles on its head. *Goldsmith.*

Care keeps his watch in every old man's eye. *Shakespeare.*

When men grow virtuous in their old age, they are merely
making a sacrifice to God of the Devil's leavings. *Swift.*

Last scene of all
That ends this strange, eventful history,
Is second childishness, and mere oblivion;
Sans teeth, sans eyes, sans taste, sans everything.
Shakespeare.

These old fellows have
Their ingratitude in them hereditary;
Their blood is caked, 'tis cold, it seldom flows;
'Tis lack of kindly warmth, they are not kind,
And nature, as it grows toward earth,
Is fashion'd for the journey—dull and heavy.   *Shakespeare.*
Every man desires to live long; but no man would be old.
                                                              Swift.

Age is a tyrant, who forbids, at the penalty of life, all the
pleasures of youth.   *La Rochefoucauld.*

AMBITION.

Ambition is an idol, on whose wings
Great minds are carried only to extreme;
To be sublimely great or to be nothing.   *Southey*

O cursed ambition, thou devouring bird.
How dost thou from the field of honesty
Pick every grain of profit or delight,
And mock the reaper's toil!   *Havard.*

What is ambition? 'Tis a glorious cheat.
Angels of light walk not so dazzlingly
The sapphire walls of heaven.   *Willis.*

          Dream after dream ensues,
And still they dream that they shall still succeed,
And still are disappointed.   *Cowper.*

Ambition's like a circle on the water,
Which never ceases to enlarge itself,
'Till by broad spreading it disperse to nought.
                                             Shakespeare.

          Accurst ambition,
How dearly I have bought you.   *Dryden.*

Airy ambition, soaring high.   *Sheffield.*

Why dost thou court that baneful pest, ambition? *Potter.*

——brave thirst of fame his bosom warms.   *Churchill.*

7

Ah! curst ambition! to thy lures we owe,
All the great ills that mortals bear below.   *Teckell.*

The dropsy'd thirst of empire, wealth or fame.   *Nugent.*

The glorious frailty of the noble mind.   *Hoole.*

No bounds his headlong, vast ambition knows.   *Rowe.*

Ambition is like love, impatient
Both of delays and rivals.   *Denham.*

————ambition, idly vain;
Revenge and malice swell her train.   *Penrose.*

Vaulting ambition which o'erleaps itself.   *Shakespeare.*

What's all the gaudy glitter of a crown?
What but the glaring meteor of ambition,
That leads the wretch benighted in his errors,
Points to the gulf and shines upon destruction?   *Brooke.*

Who soars too near the sun, with golden wings,
Melts them; to ruin his own fortune brings.   *Shakespeare.*

Farewell, a long farewell, to all my greatness!
This is the state of man. To-day he puts forth
The tender leaves of hope; to-morrow blossoms,
And bears his blushing honors thick upon him;
The third day comes a frost, a killing frost.   *Shakespeare.*

              'Tis a common proof,
That lowliness is young ambition's ladder,
Wherto the climber-upward turns his face;
But when he once attains the utmost round,
He then unto the ladder turns his back,
Looks in the clouds, scorning the base degrees
By which he did ascend.   *Shakespeare.*

Ambition is a lust that's never quenched.
Grows more inflamed, and madder by enjoyment.
                                                     Otway.

A slave has but one master; the ambitious man has as
many masters as there are persons whose aid may contribute to
the advancement of his fortune.   *La Bruyère.*

Our natures are like oil; compound us with anything,
Yet will we strive to swim at the top.

Beaumont and Fletcher.

Dreams, indeed, are ambition; for the very substance of the ambitious is merely the shadow of a dream. And I hold ambition of so airy and light a quality, that it is but a shadow's shadow. *Shakespeare.*

Oh, sons of earth! attempt ye still to rise,
By mountains pil'd on mountains to the skies?
Heaven still with laughter the vain toil surveys,
And buries madmen in the heaps they raise. *Pope.*

AMUSEMENTS.

The mind ought sometimes to be amused, that it may the better return to thought, and to itself. *Phaedrus.*

ANCESTRY.

I am one
Who finds within me a nobility
That spurns the idle pratings of the great,
And their mean boast of what their fathers were,
While they themselves are fools effeminate,
The scorn of all who know the worth of mind
And virtue. *Percival.*

The man who has not anything to boast of but his illustrious ancestors, is like a potato—the only thing belonging to him is under ground. *Sir T. Overbury.*

ANGELS.

So dear to heaven is saintly chastity,
That when a soul is found sincerely so
A thousand liveried angels lackey her. *Milton.*

Man hath two attendant angels
    Ever waiting by his side,
With him wheresoe'r he wanders,
    Wheresoe'r his feet abide.

One to warn him when he darkleth,
  And rebuke him if he stray;
One to leave him to his nature,
  And so let him go his way.   *Prince.*

A guardian angel o'er his life presides
Doubling his pleasures and his cares dividing.   *Rogers.*

We are ne'er like angels 'till our passion dies.   *Dekker.*

Fools rush in where angels fear to tread.   *Pope.*

ANGER.

Be ye angry and sin not; let not the sun go down upon
your wrath.   *Eph.* iv. 26.

    Anger
Is blood, pour'd and perplexed into a froth.   *Davenant.*

My rage is not malicious; like a spark
Of fire by steel inforced out of a flint
It is no sooner kindled, but extinct.   *Goffe.*

    There is not in nature
A thing that makes a man so deform'd, so beastly,
As doth intemperate anger.   *Webster's Duchess of Malfi.*

To be angry, is to revenge the fault of others upon ourselves.   *Pope.*

The intoxication of anger, like that of the grape, shows us
to others, but hides us from ourselves, and we injure our own
cause, in the opinion of the world, when we too passtionately
and eagerly defend it.   *Colton.*

When a man is wrong and won't admit it, he always gets
angry.   *Haliburton.*

My indignation, like th' imprisoned fire,
Pent in the troubled breast of glowing Aetna,
Burnt deep and silent.   *Thomson.*

If anger is not restrained, it is frequently more hurtful to
us, than the injury that provokes it.   *Seneca.*

10

O that my tongue were in the thunder's mouth!
Then with a passion would I shake the world.   *Shakespeare.*

ANGLING.

In genial spring, beneath the quiv'ring shade,
Where cooling vapors breathe along the mead,
The patient fisher takes his silent stand,
Intent, his angle trembling in his hand;
With looks unmoved, he hopes the scaly breed,
And eyes the dancing cork and bending reed.   *Pope.*

I in these flowery meads would be;
These crystal streams would solace me;
To whose harmonious, bubbling noise
I with my angle would rejoice.   *Isaac Walton.*

ANIMALS.

Let cavillers deny
That brutes have reason; sure 'tis something more,
'Tis heaven directs, and stratagems inspires
Beyond the short extent of human thought.   *Somerville.*

ANSWERING.

Any man that can write, may answer a letter.
     Shakespeare.

ANTICIPATION.

By the pricking of my thumbs
Something wicked this way comes.   *Shakespeare.*

ANTPATHY.

Some men there are love not a gaping pig;
Some that are mad, if they behold a cat.
Masterless passion sways it to the mood,
Of what it likes or loathes   *Shakespeare.*

11

ANTIQUARY.

They say he sits
All day in contemplation of a statue,
With ne'er a nose, and dotes on the decays
With greater love than the self-lov'd Narcissus
Did on his beauty.   *Shackerley Marmyon.*

ANTIQUITY.

Time's gradual touch
Has moulder'd into beauty many a tower
Which when it frown'd with all its battlements,
Was only terrible.   *Mason.*

All those things which are now held to be of the greatest
antiquity, were at one time new; and what we to-day hold up
by example, will rank hereafter as a precedent.   *Tacitus.*

ANXIETY.

It is not work that kills men; it is worry. Work is healthy;
you can hardly put more upon a man than he can bear. Worry is rust upon the blade. It is not the revolution that destroys
the machinery, but the friction. Fear secretes acids; but love
and trust are sweet juice*s*.   *Beecher.*

APOLOGY.

What! shall this speech be spoke for our excuse?
Or shall we on without apology?   *Shakespeare.*

APPEAL.

And here I stand; judge, my masters.   *Shakespeare.*

APPEARANCE.

He has, I know not what
Of greatness in his looks, and of high fate
That almost awes me.   *Dryden.*

Within the oyster's shell uncouth
  The purest pearl may hide,
Trust me you'll find a heart of truth
  Within that rough inside.   *Mrs. Osgood.*

'Tis not the fairest form that holds
  The mildest, purest soul within;
'Tis not the richest plant that holds
  The sweetest fragrance in.   *Dawes.*

APPEARANCES.

    Appearances deceive
And this one maxim is a standing rule:
Men are not what they seem.   *Harvard.*

The ass is still an ass, e'en though he wears a lion's hide.
The chameleon may change its color, but it is the chameleon still.

The world is still deceived by ornament.
In law, what plea so tainted and corrupt.
But being seasoned with a gracious voice,
Obscures the show of error? In religion,
What damn'd error, but some sober brow
Will bless it and approve it with a text,
Hiding the grossness with fair ornament?
There is no vice so simple, but assumes
Some mark of virtue on its outward parts.
How many cowards, whose hearts are all as false
As stairs of sand, wear yet upon their chins
The beards of Hercules, and frowning Mars;
Who inward search'd have livers white as milk?
And these assume but valor's excrement,
To render them redoubted. Look on beauty,
And you shall see 'tis purchas'd by the weight;
Which therein works a miracle in nature,
Making them lightest that wear most of it.
So are those crisped, snaky, golden locks,
Which make such wanton gambols with the wind,
Upon supposed fairness, often known
To be the dowry of a second head,

13

The skull that bred them, in the sepulchre.
Thus ornament is but the guilded shore
To the most dangerous sea; the beauteous scarf
Veiling an Indian beauty; in a word,
The seeming truth which cunning times put on
To entrap the wisest.   *Shakespeare.*

APPETITE.

Now good digestion wait on appetite,
And health on both.   *Shakespeare.*

APPLAUSE.

Applause is the spur of noble minds, the end and aim of
weak ones.   *Colton.*

APPLE.

He kept him as the apple of his eye.   *Deut.* xxxii, 10.

APPRECIATION.

A primrose on the river's brim,
    Or by the cottage door,
A yellow primrose was to him,
    And it was nothing more.   *Wordsworth.*

APPREHENSIONS.

Better to be despised for too anxious apprehensions, than
ruined by too confident a security.   *Burke.*

APPROPRIATION.

It is a special trick of low cunning to squeeze out knowledge from a modest man, who is eminent in any science, and
then to use it as legally acquired, and pass the source in total
silence.   *Horace Walpole.*

14

APTITUDE.

I cannot draw a cart, nor eat dried oats;
If it be man's work I will do it.   *Shakespeare.*

ARCHITECT.

Every man is the architect of his own fortune.
                                    Appius Claudius.

ARCHITECTURE.

Architecture is the printing press of all ages, and gives a
history of the state of the society in which it was erected.
                                    Lady Morgan.

ARGUMENT.

Who shall decide when doctors disagree,
And sound casuists doubt like you and me?   *Pope.*

The Devil can quote scripture for his purpose.

                                    Shakespeare.

Be calm in arguing; for fierceness makes
Error a fault, and truth discourtesy.
Why should I feel another man's mistakes
More than his sickness or poverty?
In love I should; but anger is not love,
Nor wisdom neither; therefore gently move.
Calmness is great advantage; he that lets
Another chafe may warm him at his fire,
Mark all his wand'rings and enjoy his frets,
As cunning fencers suffer heat to tire.   *Herbert.*

A man convinced against his will
Is of the same opinion still.   *Butler.*

No argument can be drawn from the abuse of a thing
against its use.   *Latin.*

In arguing, too, the parson owned his skill,
For even tho' vanquish'd he could argue still. *Goldsmith.*

15

He'd undertake to prove, by force
  O' argument, a man's no horse.
He'd prove a buzzard is no fowl,
And that a lord may be an owl,
A calf an alderman, a goose a justice,
And rooks committeemen and trustees.   *Butler.*

ARGUMENTS.

Examples I could cite you more;
But be contented with these four;
For when one's proofs are aptly chosen
Four are as valid as four dozen.   *Prior.*

ARMY.

All in a moment through the gloom were seen
Ten thousand banners rise into the air,
With orient colors waving: With them rose
A forest huge of spears, and thronging helms
Appear'd, and serried shields and thick array
Of depth immeasurable.   *Milton.*

ARTIFICE.

It is sometimes necessary to play the fool to avoid being deceived by cunning men.   *La Rochefoucauld.*

ARTIST.

A flattering painter, who made it his care
To draw men as they ought to be, not as they are.
      Goldsmith.

ASCENDENCY.

Whatever natural right men have to freedom and independency, it is manifest that some men have a natural ascendency over others.   *Greville.*

ASPECT.

The tartness of his face sours ripe grapes. *Shakespeare.*

ASSERTIONS.

There is nothing as cheap and weak in debate as assertion that is not backed by fact.

ASSIGNATION.

An assignation sweetly made,
With gentle whispers in the dark.   *Francis.*

ASSOCIATES.

Choose the company of your superiors, whenever you can have it; that is the right and true pride.   *Lord Chesterfield.*

He who comes from the kitchen, smells of its smoke; and he who adheres to a sect, has something of its cant; the college air pursues the student; and dry inhumanity him who herds with literary pedants.   *Lavater.*

ASSOCIATIONS.

There's not a wind but whispers of thy name;
And not a flow'r that grows beneath the moon,
But in its hues and fragrance tells a tale
Of thee, my love.   *Barry Cornwall.*

ASTONISHMENT.

I could a tale unfold, whose lightest word
Would harrow up thy soul; freeze thy young blood;
Make thy two eyes, like stars, start from their spheres;
Thy knotted and combined locks to part,
And each particular hair to stand on end,
Like quills upon the fretful porcupine.   *Shakespeare.*

ASTRONOMY.

The contemplation of celestial things will make a man both speak and think more sublimely and magnificently when he descends to human affairs.   *Cicero.*

ATHEISM.

Atheism is the result of ignorance and pride; of strong sense and feeble reasons; of good eating and ill-living. It is the plague of society, the corrupter of manners, and the underminer of property.   *Jeremy Collier.*

There is no being eloquent for atheism. In that exhausted receiver the mind cannot use its wings—the clearest proof that it is out of its element.   *Hare.*

Atheism is rather in the life than in the heart of man.
                    Bacon.

ATHEIST.

No atheist, as such, can be a true friend, an affectionate relation, or a loyal subject.   *Dr. Bentley.*

By night an atheist half believes a God.   *Young.*

ATMOSPHERE.

When you find that flowers and shrubs will not endure a certain atmosphere, it is a very significant hint to the human creature to remove out of that neighborhood.   *Mayhew.*

ATTENTION.

Lend thy serious hearing to what I shall unfold.
                    Shakespeare.

AUTHOR.

Never write on a subject without having first read yourself full on it; and never read on a subject 'till you have thought yourself hungry on it.   *Richter.*

If an author write better than his contemporaries, they will term him a plagiarist; if as well, a pretender; but if worse, he may stand some chance of commendation as a genius of some promise, from whom much may be expected by a due attention to their good counsel and advice.   *Colton.*

AUTHORITY.

Man, proud man!
Drest in a little brief authority,
Most ignorant of what he's most assur'd,
His glassy essence, like an angry ape,
Plays such fantastic tricks before high heaven
As makes the angels weep.   *Shakespeare.*

Authority intoxicates,
And makes mere sots of magistrates.
The fumes of it invade the brain,
And make men giddy, proud and vain;
By this the fool commands the wise
The noble with the base complies.
The sot assumes the rule of wit,
And cowards make the base submit.   *Butler.*

AUTHORSHIP.

The two most engaging powers of an author are to make *new* things *familiar,* and *familiar* things *new.*   *Johnson.*

None but an author knows an author's cares,
Or fancy's fondness for the child she bears.   *Cowper.*

'Tis pleasant, sure, to see one's name in print;
A book's a book, although there's nothing in't.   *Byron.*

AUTUMN.

Then came the autumne, all in yellow clad,
As though he joy'd in his plenteous store,
Laden with fruits that made him laugh, full glad
That he had banished hunger, which tofore
Had by the belly oft him pinched sore;

19

Upon his head a wreath that was enrol'd
With ears of corne of every sort, he bore,
And in his hand a sickle did he holde,
To reape the ripened fruit the which the earth had yold.
Spenser.

Thrice happy time,
Best portion of the various year, in which
Nature rejoiceth, smiling on her works
Lovely, to full perfection wrought.   *Phillips.*

AVARICE.

It may be remarked for the comfort of honest poverty, that
avarice reigns most in those who have but few good qualities to
recommend them. This is a weed that will grow in a barren
soil.   *Hughes.*

Because men believe not in Providence, therefore they do
so greedily scrape and hoard. They do not believe in any reward for charity, therefore they will part with nothing. *Barrow.*

O, cursed love of gold; when for thy sake,
The fool throws up his interest in both worlds,
First starved in this, then damnd'd in that to come. *Blair.*

Extreme avarice is nearly always mistaken; there is no passion which is oftener further away from the mark, nor upon
which the present has so much power to the prejudice of the
future.   *La Rochefoucauld.*

Avarice is always poor, but poor by her own fault.
Johnson.

'Tis strange the miser should his cares employ
To gain those riches he can ne'er enjoy.   *Pope.*

AVERSION.

I do not love thee, Doctor Fell.
The reason why, I cannot tell;
But this alone I know full well
I do not love thee, Doctor Fell.   *Tom Brown.*

20

AWKWARDNESS.

Not all the pumice of the polish'd town
Can smooth the roughness of the barnyard clown;
Rich, honor'd, titled, he betrays his race
By this one mark he's awkward in his face.   *Holmes.*

AXE.

When I see a merchant over-polite to his customer, begging
them to take a little brandy, and throwing his goods on the
counter, thinks I, that man has an axe to grind.
Franklin(Poor Richard.)

BABBLER.

Fie! what a spendthrift he is of his tongue!   *Shakespeare.*

BADNESS.

Damnable, both sides rogue.   *Shakespeare.*

BAG.
It is hard for an empty bag to stand upright.
Franklin (Poor Richard.)

BALL.

A thousand hearts beat happily; and when
    Music arose with its voluptuous swell
Soft eyes looked love to eyes that spake again,
    And all went merry as a marriage bell.   *Byron.*

I saw her at a country ball,
    There, when the sound of flute and fiddle,
Gave signal sweet in that old hall,
    Of hands across and down the middle.
Her's was the subtlest spell by far
    Of all that sets young hearts romancing;
She was our queen, our rose, our star;
    And when she danced—oh, heaven, her dancing   *Praed.*

BALLADS.

I knew a very wise man that believed that, if a man were permitted to make all the ballads, he need not care who should make the laws of a nation.   *Fletcher of Saltoun.*

BALLOT.

As lightly falls
As snow flakes fall upon the sod,
But executes a freeman's will,
As lightning does the will of God.   *Halleck.*

BANISHMENT.

All places that the eye of heaven visits,
Are, to a wise man, ports and happy havens.
Teach thy necessity to reason thus:
There is no virtue like necessity.   *Shakespeare.*

BANQUET.

A table richly spread in regal mode,
With dishes piled, and meats of noblest sort,
And savor; beasts of chase, or fowl of game,
In pastry built, or from the spit, or boil'd
Gris-amber-steam'd; all fish from sea or shore,
Freshet or purling brook, for which was drain'd
Pontus, and Lucrine bay, and Afric coast.   *Milton.*

BASHFULLNESS.

So sweet the blush of bashfulness
Even pity scarce can wish it less.   *Byron.*

There are two distinct sorts of what we call bashfulness; *this,* the awkwardness of a booby, which a few steps into the world will convert into the pertness of a cox comb; *that,* a consciousness, which the most delicate feelings produce, and the most extensive knowledge cannot always remove.   *Mackenzie.*

BATTLE.

His back against a rock he bore.
And firmly placed his foot before;
"Come one, come all! this rock shall fly
From its firm base as soon as I." *Scott.*

Now night her course began, and over heaven
Inducing darkness, grateful truce, impos'd
Her silence on the odious din of war;
Under her cloudy covert hath retired
Victor and vanquish'd. *Milton.*

Hark! the death - denouncing trumpet sounds
The fatal charge, and shouts proclaim the onset;
Destruction rushes dreadful to the field,
And bathes itself in blood; havoc let loose
Now undistinguish'd rages all around,
While ruin, seated on her dreary throne,
Sees the plain strewed with subjects truly hers,
Breathless and cold. *Harvard.*

That awful pause, dividing life from death,
Struck for an instant on the hearts of men,
Thousands of whom were drawing their last breath!
A moment all will be life again.
*   *   *   *   *   *   one moment more,
The death-cry drowning in the battle's roar. *Byron.*

This day hath made
Much work for tears in many an English mother,
Whose sons lie scatter'd on the bleeding ground;
Many a widow's husband groveling lies,
Coldly embracing the discolor'd earth. *Shakespeare.*

When Greeks join'd Greeks, then was the tug of war;
The labour'd battle sweat, and conquest bled. *Lee.*

BEARD.

It has no bush below;
Marry a little wool, as much as an unripe
Peach doth wear;

23

Just enough to speak him drawing towards a man.

Suckling.

He that hath a beard is more than a youth;
And he that hath none is less than a man. *Shakespeare.*

BEAUTIFUL.

The beautiful are never desolate,
But some one always loves them. *Bailey.*

BEAUTY.

O she is all perfection,
All that the blooming earth can send forth fair,
All that the gaudy heavens could drop down glorious. *Lee.*

When I approach
Her loveliness, so absolute she seems,
And in herself complete, so well to know
Her own, that what she wills to do or say,
Seems wisest, virtuousest, discretest, best;
All higher knowledge in her presence falls
Degraded. Wisdom in discourse with her
Loses, discount'nanc'd, and like folly shows. *Milton.*

Nature was here to lavish of her store,
That she bestow'd until she had no more. *Brown.*

Oh! she has a beauty might ensnare
A conqueror's soul, and make him leave his crown
At random, to be scuffled for by slaves. *Otway.*

Grace was in all her steps, heav'n in her eye,
In every gesture dignity and love. *Milton.*

Beauty is a witch,
Against whose charms faith melteth into blood.

Shakespeare.

Her eyes, her lips, her cheeks, her shapes, her
features,
Seem to be drawn by love's own hand; by love
Himself in love. *Dryden.*

24

The criterion of true beauty is, that it increases on examination; of false, that it lessens. There is something, therefore, in true beauty that corresponds with the right reason, and it is not merely the creature of fancy.   *Greville.*

Beauty, like ice, our footing does betray;
Who can tread sure on the smooth, slippery way?
Pleased with the surface, we glide swiftly on,
And see the dangers that we cannot shun.   *Dryden.*

I long not for the cherries on the tree,
So much as those which on a lip I see;
And more affection bear I to the rose
That in a cheek than in a garden grows.   *Randolph.*

A thing of beauty is a joy forever,
Its loveliness increases; it will never
Pass into nothingness.   *Keats.*

O fatal beauty! why art thou bestow'd
On hapless woman still to make her wretched!·
Betray'd by thee, how many are undone.   *Patterson.*

For her own person,
It beggar'd all description; she did lie
In her pavilion,
O'er-picturing that Venus, where we see
The fancy outwork nature.   *Shakespeare.*

That is the best part of beauty which a picture cannot express.   *Bacon.*

Beauty is worse than wine; it intoxicates both the holder and beholder.   *Zimmerman.*

Beauty is truth, truth beauty—that is all
Ye know on earth, and all ye need to know.   *Keats.*

When I forget that the stars shine in air,
When I forget that beauty is in stars—
Shall I forget thy beauty.   *Thomson.*

But then her face
So lovely, yet so arch, so full of mirth.
The overflowings of an innocent heart.   *Rogers.*

All orators are dumb when beauty pleadeth. *Shakespeare.*

Socrates called beauty, a short lived tyranny; Plato, a privilege of nature; Theophrastes, a silent cheat; Theocritus, a delightful prejudice; Carneades, a solitary kingdom: Domitian said that nothing was more grateful; Aristotle affirmed that beauty was better than all the letters of recommendation in the world; Homer, that 'twas a glorious gift of nature; and Ovid, alluding to him, calls it a favor bestowed by the Gods.

Remember if you marry for beauty, thou bindest thyself all thy life for that which, perchance, will neither last nor please thee one year: and when thou hast it, it will be to thee of no price at all. *Raleigh.*

Without the smile from partial beauty won,
O, what were man! a world without a sun! *Campbell.*

Beauty,
That transitory flower; even while it lasts
Palls on the roving sense, when held too near,
Or dwelling there too long; by fits it pleases,
And smells at distance best; its sweets familiar
By frequent converse, soon grow dull and cloy you.

Jeffry.

The mate for beauty should be a man and not a money chest. *Bulwer.*

Ye tradeful merchants that with weary toil,
Do seek most precious things to make you gaine,
And both the Indies of their treasures spoil;
What needeth you to seek so far in vain?
For lo! my love doth in herself contain
All this world's riches that may far be found;
If saphyrs, lo! her eyes be saphyrs plain;
If rubies, lo her lips be rubies sound;
If pearls, her teeth be pearls, both pure and round;
If ivory, her forehead's ivory I ween;
If gold, her locks are finest gold on ground;
If silver, her fair hands are silver sheen;
But that which fairest is, but few behold,
Her mind, adorn'd with virtues manifold. *Spenser.*

26

Every trait of beauty may be traced to some virtue, as to innocence, candour, generosity, modesty, and heroism.

St. Pierre.

Beauty is but a vain and doubtful good,
A shining gloss, that fadeth suddenly,
A flower that dies when first it 'gins to bud,
A brittle glass, that's broken presently;
A doubtful good, a gloss a glass, a flower,
Lost, faded, broken, dead within an hour. *Shakespeare.*

Beauty is as summer fruits, which are easy to corrupt and cannot last; and for the most part it makes a dissolute youth, and an age a little out of countenance; but if it light well, it makes virtue shine and vice blush. *Bacon.*

Honesty coupled to beauty, is to have honey sauce to sugar.

Shakespeare.

What is beauty? Not the show
Of shapely limbs and features. No;
These are but flowers
That have their dated hours,
To breathe their momentary sweets and go.
'Tis the stainless soul within
That outshines the fairest skin. *Sir A. Hunt.*

Beauty, without virtue, is like a flower without perfume.

From the French.

BED.

Bed is a bundle of paradoxes; we go to it with reluctance, yet we quit it with regret; and we make up our minds every night to leave it early, but we make up our bodies every morning to keep it late. *Colton.*

BED-CHAMBER.

Sweet pillows, sweetest bed;
A chamber deaf to noise, and blind to light;
A rosy garland, and a weary head. *Sir Philip Sydney.*

BEE.

How doth the little busy bee
  Improve each shining hour,
And gather honey all the day
  From every opening flower.   *Watts.*

Many colored, sunshine loving, spring-betokening bee!
Yellow bee, so mad for love of early blooming flowers!
Till thy waxen cells be full, fair fall thy work and thee,
Buzzing round the sweetly-smelling garden plots and flow-
    ers.   *Professor Wilson.*

BEES.

Even bees, the little alms-men of spring bowers,
Know there is richest juice in poison-flowers.   *Keats.*

    So work the honey-bees;
Creatures, that by a rule in nature teach
The art of order to a peopled kingdom.
They have a king and officers of sorts;
Where some, like magistrates, correct at home;
Others, like merchants, venture trade abroad;
Others, like soldiers, armed in their stings,
Make boot upon the summer's velvet buds;
Which pillage they, with merry march, bring home,
To the tent royal of their emperor;
Who, busied in his majesty, surveys
The singing masons building roofs of gold;
The civil citizens kneading up the honey;
The poor mechanic porters crowding in
Their heavy burdens at his narrow gate;
The sad-ey'd justice, with his surly hum,
Delivering o'er to executors pale
The lazy yawning drone.   *Shakespeare.*

BEGGAR.

The beggar, as he stretch'd his shrivel'd hand,
Rais'd not his eyes and those who dropp'd the mite
Pass'd on unnoticed.   *Bailey.*

28

The adage must be verified—
That beggars mounted, run their horse to death.

Shakespeare.

Well, while I am a beggar, I will rail,
And say,—there is no sin, but to be rich;
And being rich my virtue then shall be,
To say,—there is no vice but beggary.   *Shakespeare.*

BEHAVIOR.

Levity of behavior is the bane of all that is good and virtuous.   *Seneca.*

What is becoming is honorable, and what is honorable is becoming.   *Tully.*

Never put off till to-morrow what you can do today.
Never trouble another for what you can do yourself.
Never spend your money before you have it.
Never buy what you do not want because it is cheap.
Pride costs us more than hunger, thirst, and cold.
We seldom repent having eaten too little.
Nothing is troublesome that we do willingly.
How much pain the evils have cost us that have never happened!
Take things always by the smooth handle.
When angry, count ten before you speak: if very angry, a hundred.   *Jefferson.*

BELIEF.

'Tis with our judgments as our watches; none
Are just alike, yet each believes his own.   *Pope.*

You believe that easily which you hope for earnestly.

Terence.

BELLS.

How soft the music of those village bells,
Falling at intervals upon the ear

In cadence sweet! now dying all **away,**
Now pealing loud again and louder still,
Clear and sonorous as the gale comes on,
With easy force it opens all the cells
Where memory slept. *Cowper.*

BENEFACTOR.

And he gave it for his opinion, that whoever could make two ears of corn, or two blades of grass to grow upon a spot of ground, where only one grew before, would deserve better of mankind, and do more essential service to his country, than the whole race of politicians put together. *Swift.*

BENEFICENCE.

Men resemble the gods in nothing so much as in doing good to their fellow creatures. *Cicero.*

BENEVOLENCE.

The conqueror is regarded with awe, the wise man commands our esteem, but it is the benevolent man who wins our affection. *From the French.*

A poor man served by thee, shall make thee rich.
Mrs. Browning.

Think not the good,
The gentle deeds of mercy thou hast done,
Shall die forgotten all; the poor, the pris'ner,
The fatherless, the friendless, and the widow,
Who daily own the bounty of thy hand,
Shall cry to heav'n and pull a blessing on thee. *Rowe.*

The truly generous is the truly wise;
And he who loves not others lives unblest. *Home.*

BIBLE.

This Book, this Holy Book, on every line,
Mark'd with the seal of high divinity,

On every leaf bedew'd with drops of love
Divine, and with the eternal heraldry
And signature of God Almighty stamp'd
From first to last; this ray of sacred light,
This lamp, from off the everlasting throne,
Mercy took down, and in the night of time
Stood, casting on the dark her gracious bow;
And evermore beseeching men with tears
And earnest sighs, to read, believe and live.   *Pollok.*

It has God for its author, salvation for its end, and truth, without any mixture of error, for its matter;—it is all pure all sincere; nothing too much, nothing wanting.   *Locke.*

The Scriptures teach us the best way of living, the noblest way of suffering, and the most comfortable way of dying.
     Flavel.

A glory gilds the sacred page,
    Majestic like the sun,
It gives a light to every age;
    It gives, but borrows none.   *Cowper.*

Within that awful volume lies
The mystery of mysteries.   *Scott.*

BIGOTRY.

She has no head, and cannot think; no heart, and cannot feel. When she moves, it is in wrath; when she pauses, it is amid ruin; her prayers are curses—her God is a demon—her communion is death—her vengeance is eternity—her decalogue written in the blood of her victims; and if she stops for a moment in her infernal flight, it is upon a kindred rock, to whet her vulture fang for a more sanguinary desolation.
     Daniel O'Connell.

To follow foolish precedents, and wink
With both our eyes is easier than to think.   *Cowper.*

BIRD.

A light broke in upon my soul—
    It was the carol of a bird;

31

It ceased—and then it came again
   The sweetest song ear ever heard.   *Byron.*

BIRTH.

When real nobleness accompanies that imaginary one of birth, the imaginary seems to mix with real, and becomes real too.   *Greville.*

BIRTHDAY.

Yet all I've learnt from hours rife,
   With painful brooding here,
Is, that amid this mortal strife,
   The lapse of every year
But takes away a hope from life,
   And adds to death a fear.   *Hoffman.*

BLESSINGS.

The dews of heaven fall thick in blessings on her.
     Shakespeare.

How blessings brighten as they take their flight!   *Young.*

BLINDNESS.

He whom nature thus bereaves,
   Is ever fancy's favorite child;
For thee enchanted dreams she weaves
   Of changeful beauty, bright and wild.   *Mrs. Osgood.*

BLOCKHEAD.

A bee is not a busier animal than a blockhead.   *Pope.*

BLUNTNESS.

       This is some fellow.
Who having been prais'd for bluntness, doth affect
A saucy roughness, and constrains the garb,

Quite from his nature: he can't flatter, he!
An honest mind and plain,—he must speak truth!
And they will take it so; if not he's plain.
These kind of knaves I know, which in this plainness
Harbor more craft, and far corrupter ends,
Than twenty silly, duckling observants,
That stretch their duty nicely.   *Shakespeare.*

I have neither wit, nor words, nor worth,
Nor actions, nor utterance, nor the power of speech,
To stir men's blood: I only speak right on.   *Shakespeare.*

BLUSHES.

The heart's meteors tilting in the face.   *Shakespeare.*

Give me the elqoquent cheek.
  When blushes burn and die
Like thine its changes speak,
    The spirit's *purity.*   *Mrs. Osgood.*

————the blush is formed—and flies—
  Nor owns reflection's calm control;
It comes, it deepens—fades and dies,
  A gush of feeling from the soul.   *Mrs. Dinnies.*

The blush is Nature's alarm at the approach of sin and her
testimony to the dignity of virtue.   *Fuller.*

Confusion thrill'd me then, and secret joy
Fast throbbing, stole its treasure from my heart,
And mantling upward, turn'd my face to crimson.
                              Brooke.

BOASTING.

When you begin with so much pomp and show,
Why is the end so little and so low?   *Roscommon.*

The empty vessel makes the greatest sound.   *Shakespeare.*

For men (it is reported) dash and vapor
Less on the field of battle than on paper.
Thus in the hist'ry of dire campaign

More carnage loads the newspaper than plain.

Dr. Wolcott.

BODY.

What! know ye not that your body is the temple of the Holy Ghost which is in you, which ye have of God: and ye are not your own? Cor. vi, 19.

For of the soul the body form doth take,
For soul is form, and doth the body make. Spenser.

BOOKS.

Books are a guide in youth, and an entertainment for age. They support us under solitude, and keep us from becoming a burden to ourselves. They help us to forget the crossness of men and things, compose our cares and our passions, and lay our disappointments asleep. When we are weary of the living, we may repair to the dead, who have nothing of peevishness, pride or design in their conversation. Collier.

Books should to one of these four ends conduce,
For wisdom, piety, delight or use. Denham.

————The place that does
Contain my books, the best companions, is
To me a glorious court, where hourly I
Converse with the old sages and philosophers;
And sometimes for variety, I confer
With kings and emperors, and weigh their counsels;
Calling their victories, if unjustly got,
Unto a strict account; and in my fancy,
Deface their ill-plac'd statues. Fletcher.

Books are men of higher stature,
And the only men that speak aloud for future times to
hear! Mrs. Browning.

Books, as Dryden aptly termed them, are spectacles to read nature. * * They teach us to understand and feel what we see, to decipher and syllable the hieroglyphics of the sense. Hare.

34

Books cannot always please, however good,
Minds are not ever craving for their food.   *Crabbe.*

He that will have no books but those that are scarce, evinces about as correct a taste in literature as he would do in friendship, who would have no friends but those whom all the rest of the world have sent to Coventry.   *Colton.*

As good almost kill a man, as kill a good book; who kills a man, kills a reasonable creature, God's image; but he who destroys a good book, kills reason itself.   *Milton.*

Reading maketh a full man, conference a ready man, and writing an exact man.   *Bacon.*

History makes men wise; poets, witty; the mathematics, subtile; natural philosophy, deep; moral, grave; logic and rhetoric able to contend.   *Bacon.*

A good book is the precious life-blood of a master spirit, embalmed and treasured up on purpose to a life beyond life.
    Milton.

'Tis in books the chief
Of all perfections to be plain and brief.   *Butler.*

Some books are to be tasted, others to be swallowed and some few to be chewed and digested.   *Bacon.*

Many books require no thought from those who read them, for a very simple reason;—they made no such demand upon those who wrote them. Those works, therefore, are the most valuable that set our thinking faculties in the fullest operation.
    Colton.

I have somewhere seen it observed, that we should make the same use of a book that the bee does of a flower: she steals sweets from it, but does not injure it.   *Colton.*

BORROWING.

Go to friends for advice;
To women for pity;
To strangers for charity;
To relatives for nothing.   *Spanish Proverb.*

I can get no remedy against this consumption of the purse; borrowing only lingers and lingers it out, but the disease is incurable.   *Spanish Proverb.*

BOTTLE.

In the bottle, discontent seeks for comfort, cowardice for courage, and bashfulness for confidence.   *Johnson.*

BOUNTY.

Such moderation with thy bounty join,
That thou may'st nothing give that is not thine.
That liberality is but cast away,
Which makes us borrow what we cannot pay.   *Denham.*

BOXES.

The four boxes that rule the world—Cartridge-box, Ballot-box, Jury-box and Band-box.

BOYHOOD.

O! enviable, early days,
When dancing thoughtless pleasure's mazes,
To care, to guilt unknown!
How ill exchang'd for riper times,
To feel the follies, or the crimes
Of others, or my own.
Ye tiny elves, that guiltless sport,
Like linnets in the bush,
Ye little know the ill ye court,
When manhood is your wish!
The losses, the crosses,
That active men engage;
The fears all, the tears all,
Of dim declining age.   *Burns.*

Ah! happy years! once more who would not be a boy.
                                                             Byron.

BRAINS.

Not Hercules
Could have knock'd out his brains, for he had none.
Shakespeare.

BRAVERY.

A spirit yet unquell'd and high,
That claims and seeks ascendency.   *Byron.*

A brave man may fall, but cannot yield.
A brave man may yield to a braver man.
None but the brave deserve the fair.   *Dryden.*

That's a valiant flea that dares eat his breakfast on the lip
of a lion.   *Shakespeare.*

He is not worthy of the honeycomb
That shuns the hive because the bees have stings.
Shakespeare.

The best hearts, Trim, are ever the bravest, replied my
uncle Toby.   *Sterne.*

Nature often enshrines gallant and noble hearts in weak
bosoms—oftenest, God bless her! in female breasts.   *Dickens.*

BREEDING.

A well-bred dog generally bows to strangers.

BREVITY.

Brevity is the soul of wit
And tediousness the outward limbs, and flourishes.
Shakespeare.

If you would be pungent, be brief; for it is with words as
with sunbeams—the more they are condensed the deeper they
burn.   *Southey.*

BRIBERY.

Who thinketh to buy villainy with gold,

Shall ever find such faith so bought—so sold.

Shakespeare.

Silver, though white,
Yet it draws black lines; it shall not rule my palm
There to mark forth its base corruption.

Middleton and Rowley

BROKEN-HEART.

The heart will break, yet brokenly live on.   *Bryon.*

BROOK.

Oh for a seat in some poetic nook
Just hid with trees and sparkling with a brook.

Leigh Hunt.

BUILDING.

Never build after you are five and forty: have five years'
income in hand before you lay a brick; and always calculate
the expense at double the estimate.   *Kett.*

BULLY.

A brave man is sometimes a desperado; a bully is always
a coward.   *Haliburton.*

BUSINESS.

A man who cannot mind his own business, is not to be
trusted with the king's.   *Saville.*

There are in business three things necessary—knowledge,
temper and time.   *Feltham.*

Never shrink from doing anything which your business calls
you to do. The man who is above his business, may one day
find his business above him.   *Drew.*

BUT.

Oh, now comes that bitter word—but
Which makes all nothing that was said before,
That smooths and wounds, that strikes and dashes more
Than flat denial, or a plain disgrace.   *Daniel.*

But yet
I do not like "but yet;" it does allay
The good precedence; fie upon "but yet";
"But yet" is as a jailer to bring forth
Some monstrous malefactor.   *Shakespeare.*

CAKE.

My cake is dough.   *Shakespeare.*

CALAMITY.

How wisely fate ordain'd for human kind
Calamity! which is the perfect glass,
Wherein we truly see and know ourselves.   *Davenant.*

The willow which bends to the tempest, often escapes better than the oak, which resists it; and so in great calamities, it
sometimes happens that light and frivolous spirits recover their
elasticity and presence of mind sooner than those of a loftier
character.   *Sir Walter Scott.*

Calamity is man's true touchstone.
          Beaumont and Fletcher.

Thus sometimes hath the brightest day a cloud;
And, after summer, ever more succeeds
Barren winter with his wrathful nipping cold,
So cares and joys abound, as seasons fleet.   *Shakespeare.*

CALM.

How calm,—how beautiful comes on
The stilly hour, when storms have gone,
When warring winds have died away

39

And clouds, beneath the dancing ray
Melt off and leave the land and sea,
Sleeping in bright tranquillity.   *Moore.*

The tempest is o'er-blown, the skies are clear,
And the sea charm'd into a calm so still
That not a wrinkle ruffles her smooth face.   *Dryden.*

CALUMNY.

False praise can please, and calumny affright
None but the vicious, and the hypocrite.   *Horace.*

Be thou as chaste as ice, as pure as snow, thou
Shalt not escape calumny.   *Shakespeare.*

CANDOR.

I hold it cowardice
To rest mistrustful where a noble heart
Hath pawn'd an open hand in sign of love.   *Shakespeare.*

The brave do never shun the light;
Just are their thoughts, and open are their tempers;
Truly without disguise they love and hate;
Still are they found in the fair face of day
And heav'n and men are judges of their actions.   *Rowe.*

In simple and pure soul I come to you.   *Shakespeare.*

CANT.

'Tis too much prov'd—that, with devotion's visage
And pious action, we do sugar o'er
The devil himself.   *Shakespeare.*

CARE.

Care keeps his watch in every old man's eye
And where care lodgeth, sleep will never lie.   *Shakespeare.*

Care is no cure, but rather a corrosive
For things that are not to be remedied.   *Shakespeare.*

Care seeks out wrinkled brows and hollow eyes,
And builds himself caves to abide in them.

Beaumont and Fletcher.

Still though the headlong cavalier,
O'er rough and smooth, in wild career,
    Seems racing with the wind;
His sad companion, ghastly pale,
And darksome as a widow's veil,
    Care keeps her seat behind.   *Horace.*

God tempers the wind to the shorn lamb.   *Sterne.*

Care that is once enter'd into the breast
Will have the whole possession ere it rest.   *Johnson.*

Man is a child of sorrow, and this world,
In which we breathe, has cares enough to plague us,
But it hath means withal to soothe these cares,
And he who meditates on others' woe,
Shall in that meditation lose his own.   *Cumberland.*

CARES.

Providence has given us *hope* and *sleep,* as a compensation for the many cares of life.   *Voltaire.*

But human bodies are sic fools,
For a' their colleges and schools,
That when nae real ills perplex them,
They make enow themselves to vex them.   *Burns.*

Although my cares do hang upon my soul
Like mines of lead, the greatness of my spirit
Shall shake the sullen weight off.   *Clapthorne.*

Quick is the succession of human events; the cares of to-day are seldom the cares of to-morrow; and when we lie down at night, we may safely say to most of our troubles, "Ye have done your worst, and we shall meet no more."   *Cowper.*

CAUSE.

A good cause makes a strong arm.
God befriend us, as our cause is just.   *Shakespeare.*

A noble cause doth ease much a grievous case.

Sir Philip Sidney.

A rotten cause abides no handling.   *Shakespeare.*

CAUSES.

Small causes are sufficient to make a man uneasy, when great ones are not in the way; for want of a block he will stumble at a straw.   *Swift.*

CAUTION.

It is a good thing to learn caution by the misfortunes of others.   *Syrus.*

All's to be fear'd where all is to be lost.   *Byron.*

More firm and sure the hand of courage strikes,
When it obeys the watchful eye of caution.   *Thomson.*

Trust none.
For oaths are straws, men's faiths are wafer cakes,
And hold-fast is the only dog.   *Shakespeare.*

Beware equally of a sudden friend, and a slow enemy.

Home.

CAUTIOUS MAN.

He knows the compass, sail, and oar
Or never launches from the shore;
Before he builds computes the cost,
And in no proud pursuit is lost.   *Gay.*

CELIBACY.

But earlier is the rose distill'd
Than that which withering on the virgin thorn
Grows, lives and dies in single blessedness.   *Shakespeare.*

CENSURE.

Horace appears in good humor while he censures, and therefore his censure has the more weight as supposed to proceed from judgment, not from passion. *Young.*

The censure of those that are opposed to us, is the nicest commendation that can be given us. *St. Evremond.*

Few persons have sufficient wisdom to prefer censure which is useful to them, to praise which deceives them.

La Rochefoucauld.

CEREMONY.

Ceremony was but devis'd at first
To set a gloss on faint deeds—hollow welcomes,
Recanting goodness, sorry e'er 'tis shown;
But where there is true friendship, there needs none.

Shakespeare.

All ceremonies are, in themselves, very silly things; but yet a man of the world should know them. They are the outworks of manners and decency, which would be too often broken in upon, if it were not for that defence, which keeps the enemy at a proper distance. It is for this reason that I always treat fools and coxcombs with great ceremony: true good breeding not being a sufficient barrier against them. *Chesterfield.*

As ceremony is the invention of wise men to keep fools at a distance, so good breeding is an expedient to make fools and wise men equal. *Steele.*

CHANCE.

A lucky chance that oft decides the fate
Of mighty monarchs. *Thomson.*

Although men flatter themselves with their great actions, they are not so often the result of a great design as of chance.

La Rochefoucauld.

As the ancients wisely say
Have a care o' th' main chance,

And look before you ere you leap;
For as you sow y'ere like to reap.   *Butler.*

Be careful still of the main chance.   *Dryden.*

CHANGE.

Ships, wealth, general confidence,—
All were his;
He counted them at break of day,
And when the sun set! where were they?   *Bryon.*

Gather ye rosebuds while ye may,
    Old Time is still a flying;
And that same flower that blooms to-day,
    To-morrow shall be dying.   *Herrick.*

CHARACTER.

Those who see thee in thy full blown pride,
Know little of affections crushed within
And wrongs which frenzy thee.   *Talfourd.*

Thou wilt quarrel with a man that hath a hair more or a
hair less in his beard than thou hast. Thou wilt quarrel with a
man for cracking nuts, having no other reason but because
thou hast hazel eyes; what eye but such an eye, would spy out
such a quarrel? Thy head is as full of quarrels, as an egg is full
of meat.   *Shakespeare.*

Those who quit their proper character to assume what does
not belong to them, are for the greater part ignorant of both
the character they leave and of the character they assume.

Burke.

He who when called upon to speak a disagreeable truth,
tells it boldly and has done, is both bolder and milder than he
who nibbles in a low voice and never ceases nibbling. *Lavater.*

Decision of character is one of the most important of human qualities, philosophically considered. Speculation, knowledge, is not the chief end of man; it is action.   *   *   * "Give
us the man," shout the multitude, "who will step forward and
take the responsibility." He is instantly the idol, the lord, and

44

the king among men. He, then, who would command among his fellows, must excel them more in energy of will than in power of intellect. *Burnap.*

Character is a perfectly educated will. *Novalis.*

Spare in diet;
Free from gross passion, or of mirth, or anger;
Constant in spirit, not swerving with the blood;
Garnish'd and deck'd with modest compliment;
Not working with the eye, without the ear,
And, but purged in judgment, trusting neither.

Shakespeare.

The best rules to form a young man are, to talk little, to hear much, to reflect alone upon what has passed in company, to distrust one's own opinions, and value others that deserve it.
Sir Wm. Temple.

Best men are often moulded out of faults. *Shakespeare.*

Every man has in himself a continent of undiscovered character. Happy is he who acts the Columbus to his own soul.
Sir J. Stevens.

The most trifling actions that affect a man's credit are to be regarded. The sound of your hammer at five in the morning, or nine at night, heard by a creditor, makes him easy six months longer; but if he sees you at a Billiard table, or hears your voice at a Tavern, when you should be at work, he sends for his money the next day. *Franklin.*

CHARACTERS.

Nature hath fram'd strange bed-fellows in her time;
Some, that will evermore peep through their eyes,
And laugh like parrots, at a bag-piper;
And other of such vinegar aspect,
That they'll not show their teeth in way of smile
Though Nestor swear the jest be laughable. *Shakespeare.*

CHARITY.

Charity suffereth long, and is kind; charity envieth not; charity vaunteth not itself, is not puffed up, doth not behave itself unseemly, seeketh not her own, is not easily provoked, thinketh no evil; rejoiceth not in iniquity but rejoiceth in the truth; beareth all things, believeth all things, hopeth all things, endureth all things.   1 *Cor*. xiii. 1.

And now abideth faith, hope and charity, these three; but the greatest of these is charity.   1 *Cor*, xiii, 13.

Gently to hear, kindly to judge.   *Shakespeare*.

Give to him that asketh thee; and from him that would borrow of thee turn not thou away.   *Matthew*.

Charity shall cover a multitude of sins.   1 *Peter* iv, 8.

He who receives a good turn should never forget it; he who does one should never remember it.   *Charron*.

The drying up a single tear has more
Of honest fame than shedding seas of gore.   *Byron*.

Charity ever
Finds in the act reward, and needs no trumpet
In the receiver.   *Beaumont and Fletcher*.

For true charity
Though ne'er so secret finds its just reward.   *May*.

A woman who wants a charitable heart, wants a pure mind.   *Haliburton*.

A physician is not angry at the intemperance of a mad patient, nor does he take it ill to be railed at by a man in a fever. Just so should a wise man treat all mankind, as a physician treats a patient, and look upon them only as sick and extravagant.   *Seneca*.

CHASTITY.

O, she is colder than the mountain's snow,
To such a subtile purity she's wrought.   *Crown*.

Chaste as the icicle
That's curdled by the frost of purest snow,
And hangs on Dian's temple.   *Shakespeare*.

46

CHEERFULNESS.

Give us, O give us, the man who sings at his work! Be his occupation what it may, he is equal to any of those who follow the same pursuit in silent sullenness. He will do more in the same time—he will do it better—he will persevere longer.

Carlyle.

A merry heart goes all the day,
A sad tires in a mile. *Shakespeare.*

Cheerfulness is health; the opposite, melancholy, is disease.

Haliburton.

CHILD.

The child is father of the man. *Wordsworth.*

How sharper than a serpent's tooth it is
To have a thankless child. *Shakespeare.*

Train up a child in the way he should go; and when he is old he will not depart from it. *Proverbs* xxii, 6.

CHILDHOOD.

Sweet childish days that were as long
As twenty days are now. *Wordsworth.*

A simple child,
That lightly draws its breath,
And feels its life in every limb,
What should it know of death? *Wordsworth.*

CHILDREN.

Fragile beginnings of a mighty end. *Mrs. Norton.*

Delightful task! to rear the tender thought,
To teach the young idea how to shoot,
To pour the fresh instruction o'er the mind,
To breathe the enlivening spirit and to fix
The generous purpose in the glowing breast! *Thomson.*

Call not that man wretched, who whatever ills he suffers, has a child to love.   *Southey.*

CHOICE.

When better cherries are not to be had,
We needs must take the seeming best of bad.   *Daniel.*

The measure of choosing well, is whether a man likes what he has chosen.   *Lamb.*

There's a small choice in rotten apples.   *Shakespeare.*

CHRIST.

Jesus Christ the same yesterday, to-day, and forever.
                                        Hebrews xiii, 8.

The best of men
That e'er wore earth about Him was a sufferer,
A soft, meek, patient, humble, tranquil spirit,
The first true gentleman that ever breathed.   *Decker.*

CHRISTIAN.

A Christian in this world is but gold in the ore; at death the pure gold is melted out and separated and the dross cast away and consumed.   *Flavel.*

A Christian is the highest style of man.   *Young.*

A Christian is God Almighty's gentleman.   *J. C. Hare.*

CHRISTIANITY.

Ours is a religion jealous in its demands, but how infinitely prodigal in its gifts! It troubles you for an hour, it repays you by immortality.   *Bulwer.*

CHURCH.

What is a church? Our honest sexton tells,
'Tis a tall building, with a tower and bells.   *Crabbe.*

Look on this edifice of marble made—
How fair it swells, too beautiful to fade.
See what fine people in its portals crowd,
Smiling and greeting, talking, laughing loud!
What is it? Surely not a gay exchange,
Where wit and beauty social joys arrange,
Not a grand shop, where late Parisian styles
Attract rich buyers from a thousand miles?
But step within; no need of further search.
Behold, admire a fashionable church!
Look how its oriel window glints and gleams,
What tinted light magnificently streams
On the proud pulpit, carved with quaint device,
Where velvet cushions, exquisitely nice,
Presse'd by the polish'd preacher's dainty hands,
Hold a large volume clasp'd by golden bands.

Park Benajmin.

CIPHERS.

There are foure great cyphers in the world; hee that is lame among dancers, dumbe among lawyers, dull among scholars, and rude amongst courtiers. Bishop Earle.

CIVILITY.

Whilst thou livest keep a good tongue in thy head.

Shakespeare.

A good word is an easy obligation, but not to speak ill, requires only our silence, which costs us nothing. Tillotson.

The insolent civility of a proud man is, if possible, more shocking than his rudeness could be; because he shows you, by his manner, that he thinks it mere condescension in him; and that his goodness alone bestows upon you what you have no pretense to claim. Chesterfield.

CLEANLINESS.

Even from the body's purity, the mind
Receives a secret, sympathetic aid. Thomson.

Let thy mind's sweetness have its operation upon thy body, clothes, and habitation.   *Herbert.*

CLOCK.

A clock! with its ponderous embowelments of lead and brass, its pert or solemn dullness of communication.   *Lamb.*

CLOUDS.

Was I deceived, or did a sable cloud
Turn forth her silver lining on the night?   *Milton.*

Those playful fancies of the mighty sky.   *Smith.*

That look'd
As though an angel, in his upward flight,
Had left his mantle floating in mid-air.   *Joanna Baillie.*

COCK.

I have heard
The cock, that is the trumpet to the morn,
Doth, with his lofty and shrill-sounding throat,
Awake the god of day.   *Shakespeare.*

COFFEE.

Coffee, which makes the politician wise,
And see through all things with his half shut eyes.   *Pope.*

COMFORT.

Sweet as refreshing dews or summer showers,
To the long parching thirst of drooping flowers;
Grateful as fanning gales to fainting swains
And soft as trickling balm to bleeding pains.
Such are thy words.   *Gay.*

I would bring balm and pour it into your wound,
Cure your distemper'd mind and heal your fortunes.

        Dryden.

Thy words have darted hope into my soul
And comfort dawns upon me.   *Southern.*

COMMANDER.

It is better to have a lion at the head of an army of sheep,
than a sheep at the head of an army of lions.   *Defoe.*

COMMENDATION.

Commend a fool for his wit, or a knave for his honesty,
and they will receive you into their bosom.   *Fielding.*

COMMERCE.

A well regulated commerce is not, like law, physic, or
divinity, to be overstocked with hands; but, on the contrary,
flourishes by multitudes and gives employment to all its professors.   *Addison.*

COMPANIONS.

The most agreeable of all companions is a simple, frank
man, without any high pretensions to an oppressive greatness;
one who loves life, and understands the use of it; obliging, alike
at all hours; above all, of a golden temper, and steadfast as an
anchor. For such an one we gladly exchange the great genius, the most brilliant wit, the profoundest thinker.   *Lessing.*

COMPANY.

No company is far preferable to bad, because we are more
apt to catch the vices of others than virtues, as disease is far
more courageous than health.   *Colton.*

Bad company is like a nail driven into a post, which, after
the first or second blow, may be drawn out with little difficulty;
but being once driven up to the head, the pincers cannot take
hold to draw it out, but which can only be done by the destruction of the wood.   *Augustine.*

Take rather than give the tone to the company you are in.

If you have parts you will show them more or less upon every subject; and if you have not, you had better talk sillily upon a subject of other people's than of your own choosing.

Chesterfield.

No man can possibly improve in any company for which he has not respect enough to be under some degree of restraint.

Chesterfield.

COMPENSATION.

When articles rise the consumer is the first that suffers, and when they fall, he is the last that gains. *Colton.*

COMPETENCE.

O grant me, heav'n, a middle state
Neither too humble or too great;
More than enough for nature's ends,
With something left to treat my friends. *Mallet.*

COMPLAINING.

I will not be as those who spend the day in complaining of the head-ache, and the night in drinking the wine that gives the head-ache. *Goethe.*

COMPLIMENTS.

Compliments of congratulation are always kindly taken, and cost nothing but pen, ink and paper. I consider them as draughts upon good breeding, where the exchange is always greatly in favor of the drawer. *Chesterfield.*

CONCEALMENT.

We shall find that it is less difficult to hide a thousand guineas than one hole in your coat. *Colton.*

To conceal anything from those to whom I am attached,

is not in my nature. I can never close my lips where I have opened my heart. *Dickens.*

CONCEIT.

Conceit is to nature what paint is to beauty; it is not only needless, but impairs what it would improve. *Pope.*

A strong conceit is rich; so most men deem;
If not to be, 'tis comfort yet to seem. *Marston.*

The more any one speaks of himself, the less he likes to hear another talked of. *Lavater.*

Conceit in weakest bodies strongest works. *Shakespeare.*

CONCEIT AND CONFIDENCE.

Success seems to be that which forms the distinction between confidence and conceit. Nelson, when young was piqued at not being noticed in a certain paragraph of the newspapers, which detailed an action wherein he had assisted, "But never mind," said he, "I will one day have a gazette of my own."
Colton.

CONCILIATION.

Agree with thine adversary quickly while thou art in the way with him. *Matt.* v, 25.

CONCLUSION.

O most lame and impotent conclusion. *Shakespeare.*

CONDUCT.

Have more than thou showest,
Speak less than thou knowest,
Lend less than thou owest,
Learn more than thou trowest,
Set less than thou throwest. *Shakespeare.*

CONFESSION.

A man should never be ashamed to own he has been in the wrong, which is but saying, in other words, that he is wiser today than he was yesterday.   *Pope.*

CONFIDENCE.

There is a kind of greatness which does not depend upon fortune; it is a certain manner that distinguishes us, and which seems to destine us for great things; it is the value we insensibly set upon ourselves; it is by this quality, that we gain the deference of other men, and it is this which commonly raises us more above them, than birth, rank, or even merit itself.

La Rochefoucauld.

CONFUSION.

Confusion now hath made his masterpiece!   *Shakespeare.*

With ruin upon ruin, rout on rout,
Confusion worse confounded.   *Milton.*

CONSCIENCE.

Suspicion haunts the guilty mind
The thief doth fear each bush an officer.   *Shakespeare.*

I feel within me
A peace above all earthly dignities,
A still and quiet conscience.   *Shakespeare.*

The torture of a bad conscience is the hell of a living soul.
Calvin.

What stronger breast-plate than a heart untainted?
Thrice is he arm'd, who hath his quarrel just;
And he but naked, though lock'd up in steel,
Whose conscience with injustice is corrupted.

Shakespeare.

My conscience hath a thousand several tongues,
And every tongue brings in a several tale;
And every tale condemns me for a villain.   *Shakespeare.*

Man's conscience is the oracle of God!   *Byron.*

Conscience has no more to do with gallantry than it has
with politics.   *Sheridan.*

Thus conscience doth make cowards of us all.
                                                         Shakespeare.

A still, small voice.   I *Kings* xix, 12.

CONSEQUENCES.

As the dimensions of the tree are not always regulated by
the size of the seed, so the consequences of things are not always proportionate to the apparent magnitude of those events
that have produced them.   *Colton.*

CONSISTENCY.

Either take Christ in your lives, or cast him out of your
lips; either be that thou seemest, or else be what thou art.
                                                         Dyer.

CONSPIRACIES.

Conspiracies no sooner should be form'd
Then executed.   *Addison.*

CONSTANCY.

There are two kinds of constancy in love, one arising from
incessantly finding in the loved one fresh objects to love, the
other from regarding it as a point of honor to be constant.
                                                    La Rochefoucauld.

I am constant as the northern star;
Of whose true fix'd and resting quality
There is no fellow in the firmament.   *Shakespeare.*

CONTEMPLATION.

There is no lasting pleasure but contemplation; all others
grow flat and insipid upon frequent use; and when a man hath

run through a set of vanities, in the declension of his age, he knows not what to do with himself, if he cannot think; he saunters about from one dull business to another, to wear out time; and hath no reason to value Life but because he is afraid of death. *Burnet.*

CONTEMPT.

Those only are despicable who fear to be despised.
La Rochefoucauld.

Despise not any man, and do not spurn any thing. For there is no man that hath not his hour, nor is there any thing that hath not its place. *Rabbi Ben Azai.*

CONTENT.

There is a jewel which no Indian mine can buy,
No chemic art can counterfeit;
It makes men rich in greatest poverty,
Makes water wine, turns wooden cups to gold,
The homely whistle to sweet music's strain;
Seldom it comes to few from Heaven sent,
That much in little—all in naught—*content*. *Wilbye.*

Poor and content is rich and rich enough;
But riches, fineless, is as poor as winter,
To him that ever fears he shall be poor. *Shakespeare.*

CONTENTMENT.

Contentment, rosy, dimpled maid,
Thou brightest daughter of the sky. *Lady Manners.*

Contentment, parent of delight. *Green.*

Contentment produces in some measure, all those effects which the alchymist usually ascribes to what he calls the philosopher's stone; and if it does not bring riches, it does the same thing, by banishing the desire of them. If it cannot remove the disquietudes arising from a man's mind, body, or fortune, it makes him easy under them. *Addison.*

Happy the man who void of care and strife,
In silken or in leather purse retains
A good old shilling.   *Goldsmith.*

As for a little more money and a little more time, why it's
ten to one, if either one or the other would make you one whit
happier. If you had more time, it would be sure to hang heavily.
It is the working man who is the happy man. Man was made
to be active, and he is never so happy as when he is so. It is
the idle man who is the miserable man. What comes of holidays,
and far too often of sight-seeing, but evil? Half the harm that
happens is on these days. And, as for money—Don't you remember the old saying, "Enough is as good as a feast"? Money never made a man happy yet, nor will it. There is nothing in its
nature to produce happiness. The more a man has, the more he
wants. Instead of its filling a vacuum, it makes one. If it satisfies
one want, it doubles and trebles that want another way. That
was a true proverb of the wise man, rely upon it: "Better is
little with the fear of the Lord, than great treasure, and trouble
therewith."   *Franklin.*

CONTIQUITY.

Speaking generally, no man appears great to his contemporaries, for the same reason that no man is great to his servants
—both know too much of him.   *Colton.*

CONVERSATION.

Speak little and well, if you wish to be considered as possessing merit.   *From the French.*

It is a secret known to but few, yet of no small use in the
conduct of life, that when you fall into a man's conversation, the
first thing you should consider is, whether he has a greater in-
clination to hear you, or that you should hear him.   *Steele.*

The fullest instruction, and the fullest enjoyment are never
derived from books, till we have ventilated the ideas thus ob-
tained, in free and easy chat with others.   *Wm. Matthews.*

Talking is a digestive process which is absolutely essential
to the mental constitution of the man who devours many books.

A full mind must have talk, or it will grow dyspeptic.

Wm. Matthews.

The first ingredient in conversation is truth, the next, good sense, the third, good humor, and the fourth, wit.

Sir. Wm. Temple.

He who sedulously attends, pointedly asks, calmly speaks, coolly answers, and ceases when he has no more to say, is in possession of some of the best requisites of man.   *Lavater.*

CONVERSER.

He is so full of pleasant anecdote;
So rich, so gay, so poignant in his wit,
Time vanishes before him as he speaks,
And ruddy morning through the lattice peeps
Ere night seems well begun.   *Joanna Baillie.*

COQUETTE.

There affectation, with a sickly mein,
Shows in her cheeks the roses of eighteen,
Practis'd to lisp and hang the head aside,
Faints into airs and languishes with pride;
On the rich quilt sinks with becoming woe,
Wrapt in a gown for sickness and for show.   *Pope.*

See how the world its veterans rewards!
A youth of frolics, an old age of cards;
Fair to no purpose, artful to no end,
Young without lovers, old without a friend;
A fop their passion but their prize a sot,
Alive ridiculous, and dead forgot!   *Pope.*

The vain coquette each suit disdains,
And glories in her lover's pains;
With age she fades—each lover flies.
Contemn'd, forlorn, she pines and dies.   *Gay.*

CORPULENCE.

Let me have men about me that are fat,
Sleek-headed men and such as sleep o'nights.

Yond Cassius has a lean and hungry look;
He thinks too much; such men are dangerous.

Shakespeare.

Still she strains the aching clasp
   That binds her virgin zone;
I know it hurts her, though she looks
   As cheerful as she can,
Her waist is larger than her life
For life is but a span.   *Holmes.*

CORRUPTION.

E'en grave divines submit to glittering gold,
The best of consciences are bought and sold.   *Dr. Wolcot.*

COUNTENANCE.

The countenance may be rightly defined as the title page
which heralds the contents of the human volume, but like other
title pages, it sometimes puzzles, often misleads, and often says
nothing to the purpose.   *Wm. Matthews.*

Physically, they exhibited no indication of their past lives
and characters. The greatest scamp had a Raphael face, with
a profusion of blonde hair; Oakhurst, a gambler, had the melancholy character and intellectual abstraction of a Hamlet; the
coolest and most courageous man was scarcely over five feet
in height, with a soft voice, and an embarrassed manner.

Bret Harte

            The cheek
Is apter than the tongue to tell an errand.   *Shakespeare.*

      A countenance more
In sorrow than in anger.   *Shakespeare.*

COUNTRY.

Scenes must be beautiful which daily view'd
Please daily, and whose novelty survives
Long knowledge and the scrutiny of years.   *Cowper.*

God made the country and man made the town;
What wonder then, that health and virtue, gifts
That can alone make sweet the bitter draught
That life holds out to all, should most abound,
And least be threaten'd in the fields and groves?   *Cowper.*

And see the country, far diffused around,
One boundless blush, one white impurpled shower
Of mingled blossoms; where the raptured eye
Hurries from joy to joy.   *Thomson.*

He who loves not his country can love nothing.   *Johnson.*

And lives there a man, with soul so dead
Who never to himself hath said—
This is my own, my native land!   *Scott.*

Had I a dozen sons, each in my love alike. I had rather
have eleven die nobly for their country, than one voluptuously
surfeit out of action.   *Shakespeare.*

COUNTRY LIFE.

Here too dwells simple truth; plain innocence;
Unsullied beauty; sound unbroken youth,
Patient of labor, with a little pleas'd;
Health ever blooming; unambitious toil,
Calm contemplation; and poetic ease.   *Thomson.*

How various his employments, whom the world
Calls idle, and who justly in return
Esteems that busy world an idler too!
Friends, books, a garden, and perhaps his pen,
Delightful industry enjoyed at home,
And nature in her cultivated trim,
Dressed to his taste inviting him abroad.   *Cowper.*

COURAGE.

Courage consists not in blindly overlooking danger, but in
seeing it, and conquering it.   *Richter.*

The intent and not the deed

Is in our power; and, therefore, who dares greatly,
Does greatly.   *Brown.*

Most men have more courage than even they themselves
think they have.   *Greville.*

The smallest worm will turn, being trodden on;
And doves will peck, in safeguard of their brood.

                                                 Shakespeare.

I do not think a braver gentleman,
More active-valiant, or more valiant young,
More daring, or more bold, is now alive,
To grace this latter age with noble deeds.   *Shakespeare.*

                True courage scorns
To vent her prowess in a storm of words,
And to the valiant action speaks alone.   *Smollett.*

                Prithee peace:
I dare do all that may become a man,
Who dares do more is none.   *Shakespeare.*

Rocks have been shaken from their solid base,
But what shall move a firm and dauntless mind?
                                                 Joanna Baillie.

COURTESY.

Ill seemes (say'd he) if he so valiant be,
That he would be so sterne to stranger wight;
For seldom yet did living creature see
That courtesie and manhood ever disagree.   *Spenser.*

As the sword of the best-tempered metal is the most flex-
ible; so the truly generous are the most pliant and courteous in
their behavior to their inferiors.   *Fuller.*

COURTIERS.

A toad-eater's an imp I don't admire.   *Dr. Wolcot.*

I am no courtier, no fawning dog of state,
To lick and kiss the hand that buffets me;

Nor can I smile upon my guest and praise
His stomach, when I know he feeds on poison,
And death disguised sits grinning at my table.   *Sewell.*

A mere court butterfly,
That flutters in the pageant of a monarch.   *Byron.*

COURTSHIP.

There is, sir, a critical minute in
Ev'ry man's wooing, when his mistress may
Be won, which if he carelessly neglect
To prosecute, he may wait long enough
Before he gain the like opportunity.
                    Marmion's Antiquary.

Men are April when they woo, December when they wed,
and maids are May when they are maids, but the sky changes
when they are wives.   *Shakespeare.*

Women are angels wooing;
Things won are done, joy's soul lies in the doing;
That she belov'd knows nought, that knows not this,—
Men prize the thing ungain'd more than it is.   *Shakespeare.*

Courtship consists in a number of quiet attentions, not so
pointed as to alarm, nor so vague as not to be understood.
                    Sterne.

Say that she rail; why then I'll tell her plain,
She sings as sweetly as a nightingale;
Say that she frown; I'll say she looks as clear
As morning roses, newly wash'd with dew;
Say she be mute and will not speak a word,
Then I'll commend her volubility
And say she uttereth piercing eloquence.   *Shakespeare.*

Trust me—with women worth the being won,
The softest lover ever best succeeds.   *Hill.*

That man that hath a tongue I say is no man,
Win her with gifts if she respect not words;
Dumb jewels often in their silent kind,

More quick than words do move a woman's mind.

Shakespare.

If with his tongue he cannot win a woman. *Shakespeare.*

She is a woman, therefore may be woo'd,
She is a woman, therefore may be won. *Shakespeare.*

COVETOUSNESS.

We never desire earnestly what we desire in reason.

La Rochefoucauld.

He deservedly loses his own property, who covets that of another. *Phoedrus.*

The things which belong to others please us more, and that which is ours, is more pleasing to others. *Syrus.*

COWARD.

Bold at the council board
But cautious in the field. *Dryden.*

A coward; a most devout; religious in it. *Shakespeare.*

Think him a great way fool, solely a coward. *Shakespeare.*

I know him a notorious liar,
Think him a great way fool, solely a coward.

Shakespeare.

Go—let thy less than woman's hand
Assume the distaff—not the brand. *Byron.*

Cowards fear to die; but courage stout,
Rather than live in snuff, will be put out.

Sir Walter Raleigh.

Cowards die many times before their deaths;
The valiant never taste of death but once. *Shakespeare.*

COWARDICE.

Those that fly may fight again,
Which he can never do that's slain,

Hence timely running's no mean part
Of conduct in the martial art.   *Butler.*

CREATION.

The heavens declare the glory of God, and the firmament
showeth his handiwork. Day unto day uttereth speech, and
night unto night showeth knowledge. There is no speech nor
language where their voice is not heard.   *Psalms* xix, I.

The spacious firmament on high,
With all the blue ethereal sky,
And spangled heavens, a shining frame
Their great Original proclaim.
*   *   *   *   *   *
Forever singing as they shine
The hand that made us is divine.   *Addison.*

CREDITOR.

The creditor whose appearance gladdens the heart of a
debtor, may hold his head in sunbeams and his foot on storms.
Lavater.

CREDITORS.

Creditors have better memories than debtors; and Creditors
are a superstitious sect, great observers of set days and times.
Franklin.

CRIME.

One crime is concealed by the commission of another.
Seneca.

Where have you ever found that man who stopped short
after the perpetration of a single crime?   *Juvenal.*

For he that but conceives a crime in thought,
Contracts the danger of an actual fault.   *Creech.*

Every crime
Has, in the moment of its perpetration,

Its own avenging angel—dark misgiving,
An ominous sinking at the inmost heart.   *Coleridge.*

CRITICISM.

Criticism is like champagne, nothing more execrable if bad,
nothing more excellent if good; if meagre, muddy, vapid, and
sour, both are fit only to engender colic and wind; but if rich
generous and sparkling, they communicate a glow of the spirits,
improve the taste, expand the heart, and are worthy of being
introduced at the symposium of the gods.   *Colton.*

Damn with faint praise, assent with civil leer,
And without sneering, teach the rest to sneer;
Willing to wound, and yet afraid to strike,
Just hint a fault, and hesitate dislike.   *Pope.*

Get your enemies to read your works in order to mend
them, for your friend is so much your second selve that he will
judge too like you.   *Pope.*

CRITICS.

Critics are a kind of freebooters in the republic of letters,
—who like deer, goats and divers other gramniverous animals,
gain subsistence by gorging upon buds and leaves of the young
shrubs of the forest, thereby robbing them of their verdure,
and retarding their progress to maturity.   *Washington Irving.*

A poet that fails in writing, becomes often a morose critic.
The weak and insipid white wine makes at length excellent
vinegar.   *Shenstone.*

CROWN.

Uneasy lies the head that wears a crown.   *Shakespeare.*

CRUELTY.

I would not enter in my list of friends,
(Though grac'd with polish'd manners and fine sense
Yet wanting sensibility), the man

65

Who needlessly sets foot upon a worm.
An inadvertent step may crush the snail
That crawls at evening in the public path,
But he that has humanity, forwarn'd,
Will tread aside, and let the reptile live.   *Cowper.*

CUNNING.

Cunning and treachery are the offspring of incapacity.
                                              La Rochefoucauld.

It is sometimes necessary to play the fool to avoid being deceived by cunning men.   *La Rochefoucauld.*

CUNNING AND WISDOM.

We take cunning for a sinister and crooked wisdom, and certainly there is a great difference between a cunning man and a wise man, not only in point of honesty but in point of ability.   *Bacon.*

CURIOSITY.

Inquisitive people are the funnels of conversation; they do not take in anything for their own use, but merely to pass it to another.   *Steele.*

I loathe that low vice curiosity.   *Byron.*

CURSING.

This nor hurts him, nor profits you a jot:
Forbear it, therefore; give your cause to heaven.
                                              Shakespeare.

CUSTOM.

Custom is the law of fools.   *Vanburgh.*

Custom does often reason overrule
And only serves for reason to the fool.   *Rochester.*

Custom, 'tis true, a venerable tyrant
O'er servile man extends her blind dominion. *Thomson.*

DANCING.

Dear creature! you'd swear
When her delicate feet in the dance twinkle round,
That her steps are of light, that her home is the air,
And she only "par complaisance" touches the ground.

Moore.

Her feet beneath her petticoat,
Like little mice, stole in and out,
   As if they feared the light.
And oh! she dances such a way,
No sun upon an Easter day
   Is half so fine a sight. *Suckling.*

Come, and trip it as you go,
On the light fantastic toe. *Milton.*

DANGER.

For danger levels man and brute
And all are fellows in their need. *Dryden.*

DARKNESS.

How sweetly did they float upon the wings
Of silence, through the empty-vaulted night,
At every fall smoothing the raven-down
Of darkness till it smiled. *Milton.*

Dark night that from the eye his function takes,
The ear more quick of apprehension makes,
Wherein it doth impair the seeing sense,
It pays the hearing double recompense. *Shakespeare.*

DAY.

One of the heavenly days that cannot die. *Wordsworth.*

"I've lost a day"—the prince who nobly cried
Had been an emperor, without his crown.   *Young.*

DAYBREAK.

At last the golden oriental gate
Of greatest heaven 'gan to open fair;
And Phoebus, fresh as bridegroom to his mate,
Came dancing forth shaking his dewy hair,
And hurl'd his glist'ning beams through gloomy air.

Spenser.

It was the lark, the herald of the morn,
No nightingale. Look love, what envious streaks
Do lace the severing clouds in yonder East;
Night's candles are burnt out, and jocund day
Stands tip-toe on the misty mountain tops.   *Shakespeare.*

DEAD.

Weep not for him that dieth,
    For he hath ceased from tears,
And a voice to his replieth
    Which he hath not heard for years.   *Mrs. Norton.*

All that tread
The globe are but a handful to the tribes
That slumber in its bosom. Take the wings
Of morning, and the Barcan desert pierce,
Or lose thyself in the continuous woods
Where rolls the Oregon, and hears no sound
Save his own dashings,—yet the dead are there;
And millions in those solitudes, since first
The flight of years began, have laid them down
In their last sleep; the dead reign there alone.   *Bryant.*

Duncan is in his grave;
After life's fitful fever he sleeps well;
Treason has done his worst; nor steel, nor poison,
Malice domestic, foreign levy, nothing
Can touch him further.   *Shakespeare.*

68

DEATH.

O death! the poor man's dearest friend,
　The kindest and the best!
Welcome the hour, my aged limbs
　Are laid with thee at rest *Burns.*

Let no man fear to die, we love to sleep all,
And death is but the sounder sleep. *Beaumont.*

To what base uses may we return! Why may not imagination trace the noble dust of Alexander, till it find it stopping a bunghole? As thus: Alexander died, Alexander was buried, Alexander returneth to dust; the dust is earth: of earth we make loam. And why of that loam, whereto he was converted, might they not stop a beer barrel? *Shakespeare.*

But yesterday the word of Caesar might
Have stood against the world; now lies he there,
And none so poor to do him reverence. *Shakespeare.*

Death opens the gate of fame, and shuts the gate of envy after it; it unlooses the chain of the captive, and puts the bondsman's task into another man's hand. *Sterne.*

O grave! where is thy victory?
O death! where is thy sting? *Pope.*

Whom the Gods love die young. *Byron.*

Why, what is pomp, rule, reign, but earth and dust?
And live we how we can, yet die we must. *Shakespeare.*

And thou art terrible—the tear,
The groan, the knell, the pall, the bier;
And all we know, or dream, or fear
Of agony, are thine. *Halleck.*

　　Nothing in his life
Became him like the leaving it; he died
As one who had been studied in his death,
To throw away the dearest thing he owed,
As 'twere a careless trifle. *Shakespeare.*

　　Weep not for those
Who sink within the arms of death

Ere yet the chilling wintry breath
        Of sorrow o'er them blows;
But weep for them who here remain,
The mournful heritors of pain,
Condemn'd to see each bright joy fade,
And mark grief's melancholy shade.
        Flung o'er Hope fairest rose.

                                        Mrs. Embury.

        If I must die
I will encounter darkness as a bride
And hug it in my arms.   *Shakespeare.*

        It is hard
To feel the hand of death arrest one's steps,
Throw a chill blight o'er all one's budding hopes,
And hurl one's soul untimely to the shades
Lost in the gaping gulf of blank oblivion.   *Kirk White.*

Death is but what the haughty brave,
The weak must bear, the wretch must crave.   *Byron.*

O death all eloquent, you only prove
What dust we dote on, when 'tis man we love.   *Pope.*

Neither the sun nor death can be looked at steadily.
                                La Rochefoucauld.

        To die—to sleep—
No more;—and, by a sleep, to say we end
The heart-ache, and the thousand natural shocks,
That flesh is heir to,—'Tis a consummation
Devoutly to be wish'd.   *Shakespeare.*

Leaves have their time to fall,
    And flowers to wither at the north wind's breath,
And stars to set; but all—
    Thou hast all seasons for thine own, O, death!
                                    Mrs. Hemans.

        Lay her i' the earth;
And from her fair and unpolluted flesh
May violets spring!   *Shakespeare.*

Oh my love, my wife!

Death, that hath suckt the honey of thy breath,
Hath had no power yet upon thy beauty,
Thou art not conquer'd; beauty's ensign yet
Is crimson in thy lips, and in thy cheeks,
And death's pale flag is not advanced there.
Why art thou yet so fair?   *Shakespeare.*

Pale death approaches with an equal step, and knocks
indiscriminately at the door of the cottage, and the portals of
the palace.   *Horace.*

Death's but a path that *must* be trod,
If man would ever pass to God.   *Parnell.*

It is impossible that anything so natural, so necessary, and
so universal as death, should ever have been designed by Providence as an evil to mankind.   *Swift.*

For good men but *see* death, the wicked taste it.   *Johnson.*

Death is a commingling of eternity with time; in the death
of a good man, eternity is seen looking through time.   *Goethe.*

Thou know'st 'tis common; all that live must die,
Passing through nature to eternity.   *Shakespeare.*

Early, bright, transient, chaste as morning dew,
She sparkled, was exhal'd, and went to heaven.'   *Young.*

So live, that when thy summons comes to join
That innumerable caravan that moves
To that mysterious realm, where each shall take
His chamber in the silent halls of death,
Thou go not like the quarry-slave at night,
Scourged to his dungeon; but sustain'd and sooth'd
By an unfaltering trust, approach thy grave,
Like one that draws the drapery of his couch
Around him, and lies down to pleasant dreams.   *Bryant.*

All was ended now, the hope, the fear and the sorrow,
All the aching of heart, the restless, unsatisfied longing
All the dull, deep pain, and constant anguish of patience!
                                            Longellow.

71

A sleep without dreams after a rough day
Of toil, is what we covet most; and yet
How clay shrinks back from mere quiescent clay. *Byron.*

It is not strange that that early love of the heart should come back, as it so often does when the dim eye is brightening with its last light. It is not strange that the freshest fountains the heart has ever known in its wastes should bubble up anew when the life-blood is growing stagnant. It is not strange that a bright memory should come to a dying old man, as the sunshine breaks across the hills at the close of a stormy day; nor that in the light of that ray, the very clouds that made the day dark grow gloriously beautiful. *Hawthorne.*

How wonderful is death!
Death and his brother sleep. *Shelley.*

DEBT.

Run not into debt, either for wares sold, or money borrowed; be content to want things that are not of absolute necessity, rather than run up the score. *Sir. M. Hale.*

A public debt is a kind of anchor in the storm; but if the anchor be too heavy for the vessel, she will be sunk by that very weight which was intended for her preservation. *Colton.*

DEBTOR.

The ghost of many a veteran bill
Shall hover around his slumbers. *Holmes.*

The ghostly dun shall worry his sleep,
    And constables cluster around him,
And he shall creep from the wood-hole deep.
    Where their spectre eyes have found him. *Holmes.*

DECAY.

My way of life
Is fall'n into the sear and yellow leaf. *Shakespeare.*

DECEIT.

Smooth runs the water, where the brook is deep;
And in his simple show he harbors treason.
The fox barks not when he would steal the lamb.

Shakespeare.

DECENCY.

Immodest words admit of no defence
For want of decency is want of sense.

Earl of Roscommon.

DECEPTION.

Of all the agonies of life, that which is most poignant and harrowing—that which for the time annihilates reason and leaves our whole organization one lacerated, mangled heart—is the conviction that we have been deceived where we placed all the trust of love. *Bulwer.*

No man was ever so much deceived by another as by himself. *Greville.*

The first and worst of all frauds is to cheat oneself. All sin is easy after that. *Bailey.*

DEFECTS.

If we had no defects ourselves, we should not take so much pleasure in noting those of others. *La Rochefoucauld.*

In the intercourse of life we please, often, more by our defects than by our good qualities. *La Rochefoucauld.*

DEFORMITY.

Deformity of the heart I call
The worst deformity of all;
For what is form, or what is face.
But the soul's index, or its case?

Colton.

DEGENERACY.

What a falling off was there! *Shakespeare.*

DEJECTION.

Ah, there are moments for us here, when seeing
　　Life's inequalities, and woe, and care,
The burdens laid upon our mortal being
　　Seem heavier than the human heart can bear.

Phoebe Cary.

DELAYS.

Be wise to-day, 'tis madness to defer.
Next day, the fatal precedent will plead
Thus on, till wisdom is push'd out of life. *Young.*

DELICACY.

If you destroy delicacy and a sense of shame in a young
girl, you deprave her very fast. *Mrs. Stowe.*

DEPENDENCE.

There is none made so great, but he may both need the
help and service, and stand in fear of the power and unkind-
ness, even of the meanest of mortals. *Seneca.*

Depend on no man, on no friend, but him who can depend on himself. He only who acts conscientiously towards himself will act so towards others, and vice versa. *Lavater.*

DESIRE.

O, fierce desire, the spring of sighs and tears,
　　Reliev'd with want, impoverish'd with store,
Nurst with vain hopes, and fed with doubtful fears.
　　Whose force withstood, increaseth more and more!

Brandon.

The desire of the moth for the star—

74

Of the night for the morrow—
The devotion to something afar
  From the sphere of our sorrow.   *Shelley.*

The passions and desires, like the two twists of a rope, mu-
tually mix one with the other, and twine inextricably round the
heart; producing good if moderately indulged; but certain destruction, if suffered to become inordinate.   *Burton.*

DESOLATION.

            Such a house broke!
So noble a master fallen? all gone! and not
One friend to take his fortune by the arm,
And go along with him.   *Shakespeare.*

What is the worst of woes that wait on age?
What stamps the wrinkle deeper on the brow?
To view each lov'd one blotted from life's page,
And be alone on earth as I am now.   *Byron.*

DESPAIR.

      To doubt
Is worse than to have lost; And to despair
Is but to antedate those miseries
That must fall on us.   *Massinger.*

He that despairs, degrades the Deity, and seems to intimate, that He is insufficient, or not just to his word; and in vain
hath read the Scriptures, the world, and man.   *Feltham.*

Spirits of peace, where are ye? Are ye all gone?
And leave me here in wretchedness behind ye?

                                        Shakespeare.

Beware of desperate steps!—the darkest day
Live till to-morrow, will have passed away.   *Cowper.*

        'Tis late before
The brave despair.   *Thomson.*

Talk not of comfort, 'tis for lighter ills;

I will indulge my sorrows, and give way
To all the pangs and fury of despair.   *Addison.*

DESPONDENCY.

My heart is very tired—my strength is low—
My hands are full of blossoms pluck'd before
Held dead within them till myself shall die.

                                            Mrs. Browning.

DESPOTS.

Despots govern by terror. They know that he who fears
God fears nothing else; and, therefore, they eradicate from the
mind, through their Voltaire, the Heloetius, and the rest of that
infamous gang, that only sort of fear which generates true courage.   *Burke.*

DESTINY.

The wheels of nature are not made to roll backward; everything presses on toward Eternity; from the birth of Time an
impetuous current has set in, which bears all the sons of men
toward that interminable ocean. Meanwhile Heaven is attract-
ing to itself whatever is congenial to its nature, is enriching itself by the spoils of earth, and collecting within its capacious
bosom, whatever is pure, permanent and divine.   *Robert Hall.*

DESTRUCTION.

The gates of hell are open night and day;
Smooth the descent, and easy is the way;
But to return, and view the cheerful skies,
In this the task and mighty labor lies.   *Dryden.*

DETERMINATION.

I'll speak to it though hell itself should gape,
And bid me hold my peace.   *Shakespeare.*

DEVOTION.

Private devotions and secret offices of religion are like the refreshing of a garden with the distilling and petty drops of a water-pot; but, addressed from the temple, are like rain from heaven. *Jeremy Taylor.*

DEW.

As fresh as morning dew distill'd on flowers. *Shakespeare.*

I must go seek some dew-drops here,
And hang a pearl in every cowslip's ear. *Shakespeare.*

The starlight dews
All silently their tears of love instil
Weeping themselves away, till they infuse
Deep into nature's breast, the spirit of her hues. *Byron.*

DIET.

All courageous animals are carnivorous, and greater courage is to be expected in a people, such as the English, whose food is strong and hearty, than in the half starved commonalty of other countries. *Sir Wm. Temple.*

Simple diet is best;—for many dishes bring many diseases; and rich sauces are worse than even heaping several meats upon each other. *Pliny.*

DIFFERENCES.

In differing breasts what differing passions glow!
Ours kindle quick, but yours extinguish slow. *Garth.*

DIFFICULTY.

Difficulty is a severe instructor, set over us by the supreme ordinance of a parental guardian and legislator, who knows us better than we know ourselves; and He loves us better too. He that wrestles with us strengthens our nerves, and sharpens our skill. Our antagonist is our helper. This amicable conflict with difficulty obliges us to an intimate acquaintance with our object, and compels us to consider it in all its relations. It will not suffer us to be superficial.   *Burke.*

DIGESTION.

A light supper, a good night's sleep and a fine morning have often made a hero of the same man, who, by indigestion, a restless night and a rainy morning would have proved a coward.   *Chesterfield.*

Things sweet to taste, prove in digestion sour.

Shakespeare.

DIGNITY.

True dignity is never gained by place,
And never lost when honors are withdrawn.   *Massinger.*

A fit of anger is as fatal to dignity as a dose of arsenic to life.   *Dr. Holland.*

DILIGENCE.

Who makes quick use of the moment is a genius of prudence.   *Lavater.*

DINNER.

A good dinner sharpens wit, while it softens the heart.

Doran.

DISAPPOINTMENT.

Out of the same substances one stomach will extract nourishment, another poison; and so the same disappointments in life will chasten and refine one man's spirit, and embitter another's.

Wm. Matthews.

DISCIPLINE.

Train up a child in the way he should go; and when he is old he will not depart from it.   *Prov.* xxii, 6.

Discipline, like the bridle in the hand of a good rider, should exercise its influence without appearing to do so; should be ever active, both as a support and as a restraint, yet seem to lie easily in hand. It must always be ready to check or to pull up, as occasion may require; and only when the horse is a runaway should the action of the curb be perceptible.

DISCONTENT.

Sour discontent that quarrels with our fate
May give fresh smart, but not the old abate;
The uneasy passion's disingenuous wit,
The ill reveals but hides the benefit.
                              Sir Richard Blackmore.

What's more miserable than discontent?   *Shakespeare.*

DISCRETION.

Open your purse and your month cautiously; and your stock of wealth and reputation shall, at least in repute, be great
                              Zimmerman.

There are many shining qualities in the mind of man, but there is none so useful as discretion; it is this, indeed, that gives a value to all the rest, which sets them to work in their proper times and places, and turns them to the advantage of the person who is possessed of them. Without it, learning is pedantry, and wit impertinence; virtue itself looks like weakness; the best parts only qualify a man to be more sprightly in errors, and active to his own principle.   *Addison.*

It show'd discretion, the best part of valor.
                              Beaumont and Fletcher.

Discretion in speech is more than eloquence.   *Bacon.*

DISCUSSION.

Men are never so likely to settle a question rightly as when they discuss it freely.   *Macaulay.*

Free and fair discussion will ever be found the firmest friend to truth.   *George Campbell.*

It is not the disease but neglect of the remedy which generally destroys life.   *From the Latin.*

DISHONESTY.

That which is won ill, will never wear well, for there is a curse attends it, which will waste it; and the same corrupt dispositions which incline men to the sinful ways of getting, will incline them to the like sinful ways of spending.

Matthew Henry.

Who purposely cheats his friend, would cheat his God.

Lavater.

DISTANCE.

'Tis distance lends enchantment to the view,
And robes the mountain in its azure hue.   *Campbell.*

DIVINITY.

There's a divinity that shapes our ends,
Rough-hew them how we will.   *Shakespeare.*

DOG.

Every dog must have his day.   *Swift.*

DOUBT.

When you doubt, abstain.   *Zoroaster.*

To believe with certainty we must begin to doubt.

Stanislaus.

Our doubts are traitors
And make us lose the good we oft might win
By fearing to attempt.   *Shakespeare.*

DREAMS.

Dreams are but interludes that fancy makes
When monarch reason sleeps, this mimic wakes;
Compounds a medley of disjointed things.

        *   *   *   *   *

That neither were, nor are not e'er can be.
Sometimes forgotten things, long cast behind
Rush forward in the brain, and come to mind.   *Dryden.*

            I talk of dreams;
Which are the children of an idle brain,
Begot of nothing but vain phantasy
Which is as thin of substance as the air;
And more inconstant than the wind, which woos
Even now the frozen bosom of the north,
And, being anger'd, puffs away from thence,
Turning his face to the dew dropping south.   *Shakespeare.*

DRESS.

The person whose clothes are extremely fine I am too apt
to consider as not being possessed of any superiority of fortune,
but resembling those Indians who are found to wear all the gold
they have in the world in a bob at the nose.   *Goldsmith.*

DRINKING.

The first draught a man drinks ought to be for thirst, the
second for nourishment, the third for pleasure, the fourth for
madness.

DRUNKARD.

When he is best, he is little worse than a man; and when
he is worst he is little better than a beast.   *Shakespeare.*

DRUNKENNESS.

Drunkenness is the vice of a good constitution, or of a bad memory! of a constitution so treacherously good, that it never bends until it breaks; or of a memory that recollects the pleasures of getting drunk, but forgets the pains of getting sober.
Colton.

DUTIES.

Happy the man, and happy he alone,
He, who can call to-day his own;
He who, secure within, can say
To-morrow do thy worst, for I have lived to-day.   *Dryden.*

Be not diverted from your duty by any idle reflections the silly world may make upon you, for their censures are not in your power, and consequently should not be any part of your concern.   *Epictetus.*

Stern Daughter of the Voice of God!
    O Duty! if that name thou love
Who art a light to guide, a rod
    To check the erring, and reprove;
Thou, who art victory and law,
When empty terrors overawe,
From vain temptations dost set free,
And calm at the weary strife of frail humanity!   *Wordworth.*

EAR.

One ear heard it, and at the other out it went.   *Chaucer.*

EARLY RISING.

The early morning has gold in its mouth.   *Franklin.*

Early to bed and early to rise,
Makes a man healthy, wealthy and wise.   *Franklin.*

Few ever lived to a great age, and fewer still ever became distinguished, who were not in the habit of early rising.   *Todd.*

82

EARNESTNESS.

Earnestness alone makes life eternity.   *Carlyle.*

There is no substitute for thorough going, ardent, and sincere earnestness.   *Dickens.*

EARTH.

The earth, that's nature's mother, is her tomb.

Shakespeare.

The earth is bright,
And I am earthly, so I love it well;
    Though heaven is holier, and full of light
Yet I am frail, and with frail things would dwell.

Mrs. Judson.

And fast by, hanging in a golden chain
This pendant world, in bigness as a star.   *Milton.*

EASE.

Ease leads to habit, as success to ease.
He lives by rule who lives himself to please.   *Crabbe.*

EATING.

The chief pleasure (in eating) does not consist in costly seasoning, or exquisite flavor, but in yourself. Do *you* seek sauce by sweating.   *Horace.*

The turnpike road to people's hearts I find.
Lies through their mouths, or I mistake mankind.

Dr. Wolcot.

The difference between a rich man and a poor man is this —the former eats when he pleases, and the latter when he can get it.   *Sir Walter Raleigh.*

ECCENTRICTY.

He that will keep a monkey should pay for the glasses he breaks.   *Selden.*

ECHO.

The babbling gossip of the air. *Shakespeare.*

ECONOMY.

Beware of little expenses; a small leak will sink a great ship. *Franklin.*

Economy is of itself a great revenue. *Cicero.*

EDUCATION.

A college education shows a man how little other people know. *Haliburton.*

'Tis education forms the common mind.
Just as the twig is bent, the tree's inclin'd. *Pope.*

All of us who are worth anything, spend our manhood in unlearning the follies, or expiating the mistakes of our youth. *Shelley.*

They who provide much wealth for their children, but neglect to improve them in virtue, do like those who feed their horses high, but never train them to the manage. *Socrates.*

EFFORT.

The rider likes best the horse which needs most breaking in. *Edward Garrett.*

The general prizes most the fortress which took the longest siege. *Edward Garrett.*

The vain beauty cares most for the conquest which employed the whole artillery of her charms. *Edward Garrett.*

EGOTISM.

We often boast that we are never bored, but yet we are so conceited that we do not perceive how often we bore others. *La Rochefoucauld.*

ELOQUENCE.

The clear conception, outrunning the deductions of logic, the high purpose, the dauntless spirit, speaking on the tongue, beaming from the eye, informing every feature, and urging the whole man onward, right onward, to his object,—this is eloquence, or rather it is something greater and higher than all eloquence —it is action, noble, sublime, godlike action.   *Webster.*

God gave you that gifted tongue of yours, and set it between your teeth, to make known your true meaning to us, not to be rattled like a muffin man's bell.   *Carlyle.*

Pour the full tide of eloquence along,
Serenely pure, and yet divinely strong.   *Pope.*

His tongue
Dropp'd manna, and could make the worse appear
The better reason to perplex and dash
Maturest counsels.   *Milton.*

It is but poor eloquence which only shows that the orator can talk.   *Sir Joshua Reynolds.*

Her tears her only eloquence.   *Rogers.*

Whene'er he speaks, Heaven, how the list'ning throng
Dwell on the melting music of his tongue!
His arguments are emblems of his mien,
Mild but not faint, and forcing, though serene:
And when the power of eloquence he'd try,
Here lightning strikes you, there soft breezes sigh.   *Garth.*

When he spoke, what tender words he us'd!
So softly, that like flakes of feather'd snow,
They melted as they fell.   *Dryden.*

Your words are like the notes of dying swans;
Too sweet to last.   *Dryden.*

True eloquence consists in saying all that should be, not all that could be said.   *La Rochefoucauld.*

EMPIRE.

Nations and empires flourish and decay,
By turns command, and in their turns obey.   *Ovid.*

Westward the course of empire take its way,
　　The four first acts already past,
A fifth shall close the drama with the day;
　　Time's noblest offspring is the last.　　*Bishop Berkeley.*

EMULATION.

Keeps mankind sweet by action: without that
The world would be a filthy settled mud.　　*Crown.*

END.

　　　　The end crowns all;
And that old common arbitrator, time,
Will one day end it.　　*Shakespeare.*

All's well that ends well, still the finis is the crown.

Shakespeare.

ENDURANCE.

He conquers who endures.　　*Persius.*

ENEMIES.

　　If you want enemies excel others; if you want friends let
others excel you.　　*Colton.*

The fine and noble way to kill a foe
Is not to kill him; you with kindness may
So change him, that he shall cease to be so;
Then he's slain.　　*Aleyn.*

There's not so much danger
In a known foe as a suspected friend.　　*Nabb.*

ENNUI.

Give me to drink, Mandragora,
That I may sleep away this gap of time.　　*Shakespeare.*

ENTHUSIASM.

Nothing is so contagious as enthusiasm; it is the real allegory of the tale of Orpheus; it moves stones, it charms brutes. Enthusiasm is the genius of sincerity, and truth accomplishes no victories without it.   *Bulwer.*

ENTHUSIAST.

No wild enthusiast ever yet could rest
'Till half mankind were like himself possess'd.   *Cowper.*

ENTREATY.

Once more into the breach, dear friends, once more!
                                                    Shakespeare.

ENVY.

The most certain sign of being born with great qualities is to be born without envy.   *La Rochefoucauld.*

As rust corrupts iron, so envy corrupts man.   *Anisthenes.*

Envy is but the smoke of low estate,
Ascending still against the fortunate.   *Lord Brooke.*

Envy is a weed that grows in all soils and climates, and is no less luxuriant in the country than in the court; is not confined to any rank of men or extent of fortune, but rages in the breasts of all degrees.   *Lord Clarendon.*

He who envies another admits his own inferiority.
                                                    From the Latin.

Our envy always lasts longer than the happiness of those we envy.   *La Rochefoucauld.*

EQUALITY.

In the gates of Eternity, the black hand and the white hand hold each other with an equal clasp.   *Mrs. Stowe.*

EQUITY.

All things whatsoever ye would that men should do unto you, do ye even so to them. *Matt.* vii, 12.

ERROR.

O, hateful error—Melancholy's child!
Why dost thou show to the apt thoughts of men
The things that are not? O, Error, soon conceived!
Thou never coms't unto a happy birth.
But kill'st the mother that engendered thee. *Shakespeare.*

From the errors of others, a wise man corrects his own.
Syrus.

I will not quarrel with a slight mistake,
Such as our nature's frailty may excuse. *Roscommon.*

A man's errors are what make him amiable. *Goethe.*

The best may slip, and the most cautious fall;
He's more than mortal that ne'er err'd at all. *Pomfret.*

Great errors seldom originate but with men of great minds.
Petrarch.

Errors like straws upon the surface flow:
He who would search for pearls must dive below. *Dryden.*

ESTRANGEMENT.

There is not so agonizing a feeling in the whole catalogue of human suffering, as the first conviction that the heart of the being whom we most tenderly love is estranged from us.
Bulwer.

ETERNITY.

Eternity stands always fronting God;
A stern colossal image with blind eyes,
And grand dim lips, that murmur evermore,
"God, God, God!" *Mrs. Browning.*

None can comprehend eternity but the eternal God. Eterity is an ocean, whereof we shall never see the shore; it is a deep, where we can find no bottom; a labyrinth from whence we cannot extricate ourselves and where we shall ever lose the door.   *Boston.*

Why shrinks the soul
Back on herself, and startles at destruction?
'Tis the divinity that stirs within us;
'Tis heaven itself that points out an hereafter,
And intimates eternity to man.
Eternity, thou pleasing dreadful thought!
Thro' what variety of untry'd being
Thro' what new scenes and changes must we pass?
The wide, the unbounded prospect lies before me;
But shadows, clouds, and darkness rest upon it.   *Addison.*

ETIQUETTE.

There was a general whisper, toss, and wriggle,
But etiquette forbade them all to giggle.   *Byron.*

EVENING.

The curfew tolls the knell of parting day.
   The lowing herd winds slowly o'er the lea;
The ploughman homeward plods his weary way,
And leaves the world to darkness and to me.
Now fades the glimm'ring landscape on the sight,
   And all the air a solemn stillness holds,
Save where the beetle wheels his drony flight
   And drowsy tinklings lull the distant folds.
Save that from yonder ivy-mantled tower,
   The moping owl does to the moon complain
Of such as wand'ring near her secret bower
   Molest her ancient, solitary reign.   *Gray.*

The summer day has clos'd—the sun is set;
Well have they done their office, those bright hours,
The latest of whose train goes softly out
In the red west.   *Bryant.*

Sweet is the hour of rest,
  Pleasant the wind's low sigh,
And the gleaming of the west,
  And the truf whereon we lie.   *Mrs. Hemans.*

Now stir the fire, and close the shutters fast,
Let fall the curtains, wheel the sofa round,
And while the bubbling and loud hissing urn
Throws up a steamy column, and the cups,
That cheer but not inebriate, wait on each,
So let us welcome peaceful evening in.   *Cowper.*

            How still the evening is
As hush'd on purpose to grace harmony!   *Shakespeare.*

An eve intensely beautiful; an eve
Calm as the slumber of a lovely girl
Dreaming of hope. The rich autumnal woods,
With their innumerable shades and colorings,
Are like a silent instrument at rest:
A silent instrument—whereon the wind
Hath long forgot to play.   *Houseman.*

EVIDENCE.

Hear one side, and you will be in the dark; hear both sides, and all will be clear.   *Haliburton.*

EVIL.

He who will fight the devil with his own weapons, must not wonder if he finds him an over-match.   *South.*

The doing evil to avoid an evil cannot be good.
                                                Coleridge.

An evil at its birth, is easily crushed, but it grows and strengthens by endurance.   *Cicero.*

This is the curse of every evil deed
That, propagating still, it brings forth evil.   *Southey.*

Timely advis'd, the coming evil shun!   *Prior.*

EXAMINATIONS.

Examinations are formidable even to the best prepared, for the greatest fool may ask more than the wisest man can answer.

Colton.

EXAMPLE.

Example is a living law, whose sway
Men more than all the written laws obey.　　*Sedley.*

People seldom improve, when they have not other model but themselves to copy.　　*Goldsmith.*

EXCELLENCE.

Excellence is never granted to man, but as the reward of labor. It argues, indeed, no small strength of mind to persevere in the habits of industry, without the pleasure of perceiving those advantages which, like the hands of a clock, whilst they make hourly approaches to their point, yet proceed so slowly as to escape observation.　　*Sir Josua Reynolds.*

EXCESS.

To gild refined gold, to paint the lily,
To throw a perfume on the violet,
To smoothe the ice, or add another hue
Unto the rainbow, or, with taper-light,
To seek the beauteous eye to heaven to garnish,
Is wasteful and ridiculous excess.　　*Shakespeare.*

The desire of power in excess caused angels to fall; the desire of knowledge in excess caused man to fall; but in charity is no excess, neither can man or angels come into danger by it.

Bacon.

EXCESSES.

The excesses of our youth are drafts upon our old age, payable with interest, about thirty years after date.　　*Colton.*

EXCUSE.

An excuse is worse and more terrible than a lie; for an excuse is a lie guarded.　　*Pope.*

And, oftentimes, excusing of a fault,
Doth make a fault the worse by the excuse;
As patches set upon a little breach,
Discredit more in hiding of the fault,
Than did the fault before it was so patch'd.   *Shakespeare.*

EXERTION.

With every exertion, the best of men can do but a moderate amount of good; but it seems in the power of the most contemptible individual to do incalculable mischief.

Washington Irving.

EXPECTATION.

How slow
This old moon wanes! she lingers my desires,
Like to a stepdame, or a dowager,
Long withering out a young man's revenue.   *Shakespeare.*

EXPERIENCE.

Experience keeps a dear school, but fools will learn in no other, and scarcely in that; for it is true, we may give *advice,* but we cannot give *conduct.* Remember this; they that will not be counseled cannot be helped. If you do not hear reason she will rap you over your knuckles.   *Franklin.*

I had rather have a fool to make me merry, than experience to make me sad.   *Shakespeare.*

Ah! the youngest heart has the same waves within it as the oldest; but without the plummet which can measure the depths.
Richter.

All is but lip wisdom which wants experience.
Sir Philip Sydney.

EXTRAVAGANCE.

The man who builds and wants wherewith to pay
Provides a home from which to run away.   *Young.*

Dreading the climax of all human ills,
The inflammation of his weekly bills.   *Byron.*

EYE.

An eye like Mars, to threaten and command.   *Shakespeare.*

A beautiful eye makes silence eloquent, a kind eye makes
contradiction an assent, an enraged eye makes beauty deformed.
This little member gives life to every part about us; and I believe the story of Argus implies no more, than that the eye is in
every part; that is to say, every other part would be mutilated,
were not its force represented more by the eye than even by
itself.   *Addison.*

The eye sees not itself
But by reflection, by some other things.   *Shakespeare.*

Eyes with the same blue witchery as those
Of Psyche, which caught Love in his own wiles.
                                        From the Italian.

The soft blue eye,
That looks as it had open'd first in heaven,
And caught its brightness from the seraph's gaze
As flowers are fairest where the sunbeams fall.   *Mrs. Hale.*

His eye was blue and calm, as is the sky
In the serenest noon.   *Willis.*

A gray eye is still and sly;
A roguish eye is the brown;
The eye of blue is ever true;
But in the black eye's sparkling spell
Mystery and mischief dwell.

A pair of bright eyes with a dozen glances suffice to sub-
due a man; to enslave him and inflame; to make him even forget; they dazzle him so, that the past becomes straightway dim
to him; and he so prizes them, that he would give all his life
to possess them. What is the fond love of dearest friends compared to his treasure? Is memory as strong as expectancy,
fruition as hunger, gratitude as desire?   *Thackeray.*

Men with grey eyes are generally keen, energetic, and at

first cold; but you may depend upon their sympathy with real
sorrow. Search the ranks of our benevolent men and you will
agree with me. *Dr. Leask.*

His eyes have all the seeming of a demon's that is dreaming. *Poe.*

From women's eyes this doctrine I derive;
They sparkle still the right Promethean fire;
They are the books, the arts, the academies,
That show, contain, and nourish all the world,
Else, none at all in aught proves excellent. *Shakespeare.*

FACE.

But then her face
So lovely, yet so arch, so full of mirth,
The overflowings of an innocent heart. *Rogers.*

Her face was like an April morn,
   Clad in a wint'ry cloud;
And clay-cold was her lily hand,
   That held her sable shroud. *Mallet.*

His face was of the doubtful kind;
That wins the eye and not the mind. *Scott.*

FACTS.

One fact is better than one hundred analogies.

The right Honorable Gentleman is indebted to his memory
for his jests and to his imagination for his facts. *Sheridan.*

Facts are to the mind the same thing as food to the body.
On the due digestion of facts depends the strength and wisdom
of the one, just as vigor and health depend on the other. The
wisest in council, the ablest in debate, and the most agreeable
in the commerce of life, is that man who has assimilated to his
understanding the greatest number of facts. *Burke.*

FAIL.

Macbeth.—If we should fail—
Lady M.—We fail?
But screw your courage to the sticking place
And we'll not fail.   *Shakespeare.*

In the lexicon of youth, which fate reserves
For a bright manhood, there is no such word
As *fail*.   *Bulwer.*

There is not a fiercer hell than failure in a great object.
                                                Keats.

FAIRIES.

Did you ever hear
Of the frolic fairies dear?
They're a blessed little race,
Peeping up in fancy's face,
In the valley, on the hill,
By the fountain and the rill;
Laughing out between the leaves
That the loving summer weaves.   *Mrs. Osgood.*

                    Oft fairy elves,
Whose midnight revels by a forest side,
Or fountain, some belated peasant sees,
Or dreams he sees, while o'erhead the moon
Sits arbitress, and nearer to the earth
Wheels her pale course, they on their mirth and dance
Intent, with jocund music charm his ear;
At once with joy and fear his heart rebounds.   *Milton.*

FAIRY LAND.

Wherever is love and loyalty, great purposes and lofty souls,
even though in a hovel or a mine, there is fairy-land. *Kingsley.*

FAITH.

Faith builds a bridge across the gulf of death,
To break the shock blind nature cannot shun,

And lands thought smoothly on the further shore.   *Young.*

Nought shall prevail against us, or disturb
Our cheerful faith, that all which we behold
Is full of blessings.   *Wordsworth.*

Faith is the substance of things hoped for, the evidence of
things not seen.   *Hebrews* xi, 1.

Faith is the soul going out of itself for all its wants.   *Boston.*

Faith lights us through the dark to Deity.   *Davenant.*

For modes of faith let graceless zealots fight,
His can't be wrong whose life is in the right.   *Pope.*

Faith is not reason's labor, but repose.   *Young.*

Works without *faith* are like a fish without water, it wants
the element it should live in. A building without a basis cannot
stand; faith is the foundation, and every good action is as a stone
laid.   *Feltham.*

We should act with as much energy as those who expect
everything from themselves; and we should pray with as much
earnestness as those who expect everything from God.   *Colton.*

FALL.

I've touch'd the highest point of all my greatness.
And from that full meridian of my glory
I haste now to my setting. I shall fall,
Like a bright exhalation in the evening
And no man see me more.   *Shakespeare.*

FALSEHOOD.

A goodly apple rotten at the heart;
O, what a goodly outside falsehood hath!   *Shakespeare.*

The seal of truth is on thy gallant form,
For none but cowards lie.   *Murphy.*

A lie should be trampled on and extinguished wherever
found. I am for fumigating the atmosphere, when I suspect that
falsehood, like pestilence, breathes around me.   *Carlyle.*

96

FAME.

Fame is an ill you may with ease obtain,
A sad oppression to be borne with pain;
And when you would the noisy clamour drown,
You'll find it hard to lay the burden down.   *Cooke.*

And what is fame, that flutt'ring noisy sound,
But the cold lie of universal vogue?   *H. Smith.*

In Fame's temple there is always a niche to be found for
rich dunces, importunate scoundrels or successful butchers of
the human race.   *Zimmerman.*

Vain empty words
Of honor, glory, and immortal fame,
Can these recall the spirit from its place,
Or re-inspire the breathless clay with life?
What tho' your fame with all its thousand trumpets,
Sound o'er the sepulchres, will that awake
The sleeping dead?   *Sewell.*

I courted fame but as a spur to brave
And honest deeds; and who despises fame
Will soon renounce the virtues that deserve it.   *Mallet.*

If a man do not erect in this age his own tomb ere he
dies, he shall live no longer in monuments than the bell rings,
and the widow weeps.   *Shakespeare.*

Fame may be compared to a scold; the best way to silence her is to let her alone, and she will at least be out of
breath in blowing her own trumpet.   *Fuller.*

Fame is the spur that the clear spirit doth raise
(That last infirmity of noble minds)
To scorn delights and live laborious days;
But the fair guerdon when we hope to find,
And think to burst out into sudden blaze,
Comes the blind Fury with the abhorr'd shears,
And slits the thin-spun life.   *Milton.*

FAMINE.

This famine has a sharp and meagre face;
'Tis death in an undress of skin and bone,

97

Where age and youth, their landmark ta'en away,
Look all one common sorrow.   *Dryden.*

FANATACISM.

The Puritans hated bearbaiting not because it gave pain
to the bear, but because it gave pleasure to the spectators.

Macaulay.

FANCY.

Tell me where is fancy bred,
Or in the heart, or in the head?
How begot, how nourished?
    Reply, reply,
It is engender'd in the eyes,
With gazing fed; and fancy dies
In the cradle where it lies.   *Shakespeare.*

FAREWELL.

'Twere vain to speak, to weep, to sigh,
    Oh, more than tears of blood can tell
When wrung from guilt's expiring eye,
    Are in the word farewell—farewell.   *Byron.*

Farewell a word that must be, and hath been,
A sound which makes us linger;—yet—farewell.

Byron.

FASHION.

    Fashion, leader of a chatt'ring train,
Whom man for his own hurt permits to reign,
Who shifts and changes all things but his shape,
And would degrade her vot'ry to an ape,
The fruitful parent of abuse and wrong,
Hold a usurp'd dominion o'er his tongue,
There sits and prompts him to his own disgrace,
Prescribes the theme, the tone, and the grimace,
And when accomplish'd in her wayward school,
Calls gentleman whom she has made a fool.   *Cowper.*

I see that fashion wears out more apparel than the man.
Shakespeare.

We laugh heartily to see a whole flock of sheep jump because one did so; might not one imagine that superior beings do the same by us, and for exactly the same reason?   *Greville.*

Be neither too early in the fashion, nor too long out of it; nor at any time in the extremities of it.   *Lavater.*

FATE.

Heaven from all creatures hides the book of Fate. *Pope.*

What must be, shall be; and that which is a necessity to him that struggles is little more than choice to him that is willing.   *Seneca.*

With equal pace, impartial fate,
Knocks at the palace and the cottage gate.   *Horace.*

Fate steals along with silent tread,
Found oftenest in what least we dread;
Frowns in the storm with angry brow,
But in the sunshine strikes the blow.   *Cowper.*

FAULTS.

O wad some pow'r the giftie gie us
To see oursels as others see us!
It wad frae mony a blunder free us,
   And foolish notion.   *Burns.*

Men have many faults;
   Poor women have but two;
There's nothing good they say,
   And nothing right they do.   *Anon.*

FEAR.

In politics, what begins in fear usually ends in folly.
Coleridge.

In morals, what begins in fear usually ends in wickedness; in religion, what begins in fear usually ends in fanatacism. Fear, either as a principle or a motive, is the beginning of all evil.   *Mrs. Jameson.*

Fear is the tax that conscience pays to guilt.   *Sewell.*
The thing in the world I am most afraid of is fear, and with good reason, that passion alone in the trouble of it exceeding other accidents.   *Montaigne.*

What are fears but voices airy?
  Whispering harm where harm is not.
And deluding the unwary
  Till the fatal bolt is shot!   *Wordsworth.*

FEASTING.

It is not the quantity of the meat, but the cheerfulness of the guests, which makes the feast.   *Lord Clarendon.*

Mingles with the friendly bowl
The feast of reason and the flow of soul.   *Pope.*

FEELING.

The last, best fruit which comes to perfection, even in the kindliest soul, is, tenderness toward the hard, forbearance toward the unforbearing, warmth of heart toward the cold philanthropy toward the misanthropic.   *Richter.*

A fellow-feeling makes one wondrous kind.   *Garrick.*

FIDELITY.

Faithful found
Among the faithless, faithful only he;
Among innumerable false, unmov'd,
Unshaked, unseduced, unterrified;
His loyalty he kept, his love, his zeal
Nor number, nor example with him wrought
To swerve from truth, or change his constant mind
Though single.   *Milton.*

She is as constant as the stars

That never vary, and more chaste than they.   *Proctor.*

FINERY.

All that glisters is not gold,
Gilded tombs do worms enfold.   *Shakespeare.*

FINIS.

My pen is at the bottom of a page,
Which being finished, here the story ends;
'Tis to be wished it had been sooner done,
But stories somehow lengthen when begun.   *Byron.*

FIRE.

Behold how great a matter a little fire kindleth.

James iii, 5.

And where two raging firest meet together,
They do consume the thing that feeds their fury.

Shakespeare.

Fire that's closest kept burns most of all.   *Shakespeare.*

FIRESIDE.

The cat's Eden.   *Southey.*

FIRMNESS.

I said to Sorrow's awful storm,
    That beat against my breast,
Rage on—thou may'st destroy this form,
    And lay it low at rest;
But still the spirit that now brooks
    Thy tempest raging high,
Undaunted on its fury looks
    With steadfast eye.   *Mrs. Stoddard.*

101

FIRST AND LAST.

First must give place to last, because last must have his time to come; but last gives place to nothing, for there is not another to succeed. *Bunyan.*

FLATTERERS.

Of all wild beasts preserve me from a tyrant;
Of all tame—a flatterer. *Johnson.*

Hold!
No adulation!—'tis the death of virtue!
Who flatters is of all mankind the lowest
Save him who courts the flattery. *Hannah More.*

When flatterers meet the devil goes to dinner. *Defoe.*

FLATTERY.

Flattery is a sort of bad money, to which our vanity gives currency. *La Rochefoucauld.*

Nothing is so great an instance of ill-manners as flattery. If you flatter all the company you please none; if you flatter only one or two, you affront all the rest. *Swift.*

Sirs, adulation is a fatal thing—
Rank poison for a subject, or a king. *Dr. Wolcot.*

FOLLY.

Sick of herself is folly's character,
As wisdom's is a modest self applause. *Young.*

None but a fool is always right. *Hare.*

FOOL.

For every inch that is not fool is rogue. *Dryden.*

This fellow is wise enough to play the fool;
And, to do that well, craves a kind of wit. *Shakespeare.*

The greatest of fools is he who imposes on himself, and in his greatest concern thinks certainly he knows that which he has least studied, and of which he is most profoundly ignorant.

Shaftesbury.

Though thou shouldst bray a fool in a mortar among wheat with a pestle, yet will not his foolishness depart from him.

Prov. xxvii, 22.

FOP.

Knows what he knows as if he knew it not,
What he remembers, seems to have forgot. *Cowper.*

So gentle, yet so brisk, so wondrous sweet,
So fit to prattle at a lady's feet. *Churchill.*

The soul of this man is in his clothes. *Shakespeare.*

FORBEARANCE.

Whosoever shall smite thee on thy right cheek, turn to him the other also. And if any man will sue thee at the law, and take away thy coat, let him have thy cloak also. *Matt.* v, 39.

Use every man after his deserts, and who shall 'scape whipping. *Shakespeare.*

Everything has two handles; the one soft and manageable, the other such as will not endure to be touched. If then your brother do you an injury, do not take it by the hot hard handle, by representing to yourself all the aggravating circumstances of the fact; but look rather on the soft side, and extenuate it as much as is possible, by considering the nearness of the relation, and the long friendship and familiarity between you— obligations to kindness which a single provocation ought not to dissolve. And thus you will take the accident by its manageable handle. *Epictetus.*

FORGETFULNESS.

Of all affliction taught a lover yet
'Tis sure the hardest science to forget. *Pope.*

FORGIVENESS.

'Tis easier for the generous to forgive,
Than for offence to ask it.   *Thomson.*

FORMS.

Of what use are forms, seeing at times they are empty?—
Of the same use as barrels, which are at times empty too.   *Hare.*

FORTITUDE.

Brave spirits are a balsam to themselves;
There is a nobleness of mind that heals
Wounds beyond salves.   *Cartwright.*

——Gird your hearts with silent fortitude
Suffering yet hoping all things.   *Mrs. Hemans.*

FORTUNE.

To catch dame fortune's golden smile,
    Assiduous wait upon her;
And gather gear by every wile
    That's justified by honor.
Not for to hide it in a hedge,
    Nor for a train attendant;
But for the glorious privilege
    Of being *independent.*   *Burns.*

Fortune brings in some boats that are not steered.
                                        Shakespeare.

Fortune is like the market, where, many times, if you can
stay a little, the price will fall.   *Bacon.*

To be thrown on one's own resources is to be cast in the
very lap of fortune; for our faculties undergo a development,
and display an energy of which they were previously unsus-
ceptible.   *Franklin.*

When fortune means to men most good
She looks upon them with a threat'ning eye.   *Shakespeare.*

Fortune is merry,

And in this mood will give us anything.   *Shakespeare.*

When fortune sends a stormy wind,
Then show a brave and present mind;
And when with too indulgent gales
She swells too much, then furl thy sails.   *Creech.*

The wheel of fortune turns incessantly round, and who can say within himself, I shall to-day be uppermost.   *Confucius.*

FREE.

Who then is free? The wise man who can command himself.   *Horace.*

—— Freedom hath a thousand charms to show,
That slaves howe'er contented never know.   *Cowper.*

FRIEND.

Give me the avow'd, the erect, the manly foe,
Bold I can meet,—perhaps may turn his blow;
But of all plagues, good heaven, thy wrath can send,
Save, save, oh! save me from the candid friend.   *Canning.*

Chide a friend in private and praise him in public.   *Solon.*

To lose a friend is the greatest of all losses.   *Syrus.*

A friend to everybody is a friend to nobody.
    Spanish Proverb.

FRIENDS.

Friend after friend departs;
    Who hath not lost a friend?
There is no union here of hearts
    That hath not here its end.   *Montgomery.*

It is better to decide between our enemies than our friends; for one of our friends will most likely become our enemy; but on the other hand, one of your enemies will probably become your friend.   *Bias.*

He who hath many friends, hath none. *Aristotle.*

Old friends are best. King James used to call for his old shoes; they were easiest to his feet. *John Selden.*

Purchase not friends with gifts; when thou ceasest to give, such will cease to love. *Fuller.*

A friend in need
Is a friend indeed.

FRIENDSHIP.

So we grew together,
Like to a double cherry, seeming parted.
But yet a union in partition,
Two lovely berries moulded on one stem:
So, with two seeming bodies, but one heart. *Shakespeare.*

Friendship's the wine of life. *Young.*

We still have slept together
Rose at an instant, learn'd, play'd, eat together;
And wheresoe'er we went, like Juno's swans,
Still we went coupled, and inseparable. *Shakespeare.*

Friendship is no plant of hasty growth;
Tho' planted in esteem's deep fixed soil,
The gradual culture of kind intercourse
Must bring it to perfection. *Joanna Baillie.*

Great souls by instinct to each other turn,
Demand alliance, and in friendship burn. *Addison.*

Friendship's the privilege
Of private men; for wretched greatness knows
No blessing so substantial. *Tate.*

—— O friendship! of all things the
Most rare, and therefore most rare, because most
Excellent; whose comforts in misery
Are always sweet, whose counsels in
Prosperity are ever fortunate. *Lilly.*

Friendship is composed of a single soul inhabiting two bodies. *Aristotle.*

Friendship is the only thing in the world concerning the usefulness of which all mankind are agreed.   *Cicero.*

FRUGALITY.

Frugality may be termed the daughter of prudence, the sister of temperance, and the parent of liberty. He that is extravagant will quickly become poor, and poverty will enforce dependence and invite corruption.   *Johnson.*

FURY.

I understand a fury in your words,
But not your words.   *Shakespeare.*

FUTURE.

Heaven from all creatures hides the book of fate,
All but the page prescribed, their present fate.   *Pope.*

God will not suffer man to have the knowledge of things to come: for if he had prescience of his prosperity he would be careless; and understanding of his adversity he would be senseless.   *Augustine.*

There is no hope—the future will but turn
The old sand in the falling glass of time.   *R. H. Stoddard.*

Trust no future howe'er pleasant!
Let the dead past bury its dead!
Act—act in the living present!
Heart within and God o'erhead!   *Longfellow.*

The veil which covers the face of futurity is woven by the hand of mercy.   *Bulwer.*

GALLANTRY.

Conscience has no more to do with gallantry than it has with politics.   *Sheridan.*

Gallantry consists in saying the most empty things in an agreeable manner.   *La Rochefoucauld.*

GAMBLER.

The gamester, if he die a martyr to his profession, is doubly ruined. He adds his soul to every other loss, and by the act of suicide, renounces earth to forfeit heaven. *Colton.*

Look round the wrecks of play behold,
Estates dismember'd, mortgaged, sold;
Their owners now to jail confin'd,
Show equal poverty of mind. *Gay.*

Bets at the first were fool-traps where the wise
Like spiders lay in ambush for the flies. *Dryden.*

Some play for gain; to pass time others play
For nothing; both play the fool, I say:
For time nor coin I'll lose, or idly spend;
Who gets by play, proves loser in the end. *Heath.*

Gaming is the son of avarice, but the father of despair.

GENERAL.

A gen'ral sets his army in array
In vain, unless he fight and win the day. *Denham.*

GENEROSITY.

God blesses still the generous thought
    And still the fitting word He speeds,
And truth, at His requiring taught,
    He quickens into deeds. *Whittier.*

The truly generous is the truly wise;
And he who loves not others, lives unblest. *Horace.*

GENIUS.

The three indispensables of genius are understanding, feeling, and perseverance. The three things that enrich genius are contentment of mind, the cherishing of good thoughts, and exercising the memory. *Southey.*

No enemy is so terrible as a man of genius. *Disraeli.*

Men of genius are often dull and inert in society, as a blazing meteor when it descends to earth, is only a stone.

Longfellow.

Talent, lying in the understanding, is often inherent; genius, being the action of reason and imagination, rarely or never.

Coleridge.

There is no great genius free from some tincture of madness.
Seneca.

The greatest genius is never so great as when it is chastised and subdued by the highest reason.
Colton.

When a true genius appears in the world you may know him by this sign, that the dunces are all in confederacy against him.
Swift.

GENIUS AND TALENT.

Genius is the highest type of reason—talent the highest type of the understanding.
Hickok.

GENTLEMAN.

A gentleman has ease without familiarity, is respectful without meanness; genteel without affectation, insinuating without seeming art.
Chesterfield.

His years are young, but his experience old;
His head unmellow'd, but his judgment ripe;
And in a word (for far behind his worth
Come all the praises that I now bestow)
He is complete in feature and in mind,
With all good grace to grace a gentleman.
Shakespeare.

The grand old name of gentleman
Defam'd by every charlatan
And soil'd with all ignoble use.
Tennyson.

Education begins the gentleman, but reading, good company and reflection must finish him.
Locke.

I am a gentleman,
    I'll be sworn thou art!

Thy tongue, thy face, thy limbs, action and spirit,
Do give the five-fold blazon.   *Shakespeare.*

When Adam delved and Eve span
Who was then the gentleman?
        John Ball (revision of Hampole verse).

GENTLENESS.

Sweet speaking oft a currish heart reclaims.   *Sidney.*

GHOSTS.

Glendower.—I can call spirits from the vasty deep.
Hotspur.—Why so can I, or so can any man;
  But will they come when you do call for them?
           Shakespeare.

GIFT.

The manner of giving, shews the character of the giver,
more than the gift itself.   *Lavater.*

GIFTS.

Those gifts are ever the most acceptable which the giver
has made precious.   *Ovid.*

There is no grace in a benefit that sticks to the fingers.
           Seneca.

Your gift is princely, but it comes too late,
And falls like sunbeams on a blasted blossom.   *Suckling.*

Win her with gifts, if she respect not words;
Dumb jewels often, in their silent kind,
More quick than words do move a woman's mind.
           Shakespeare.

And with them, words of so sweet breath compos'd
As make the things more rich; their perfume lost,
Take these again; for to the noble mind

Rich gifts wax poor, when givers prove unkind.

Shakespeare.

Never look a gift horse in the mouth.　　　　*Anon.*

GLORY.

　　Real glory
Springs from the silent conquest of ourselves;
And without that the conqueror is nought,
But the first slave.　　　　*Thomson.*

Glory is the fair child of peril.　　　　*Smollett.*

Glory, the casual gift of thoughtless crowds!
Glory, the bribe of avaricious virtue!　　　　*Johnson.*

Who pants for glory finds a short repose,
A breath revives him, and a breath o'er-throws. *Pope.*

Our greatest glory consists not in never falling, but in rising
every time we fall.　　　　*Goldsmith.*

The paths of glory lead but to the grave.　　　　*Gray.*

GLUTTON.

Honor's a thing too subtle for his wisdom;
If honor lie in eating, he's right honorable.

Beaumont and Fletcher.

GLUTTONY.

Fat paunches have lean pates, and dainty bits
Make rich the ribs, but bankrupt quite the wits.

Shakespeare.

GOD.

God of my Fathers! holy, just and good!
My God! my Father, my unfailing Hope!
Jehovah! let the incense of thy praise,
Accepted, burn before thy mercy seat,
And let thy presence burn both day and night.　　*Pollok.*

A God alone can comprehend a God.   *Young.*

There is an Eye that never sleeps
   Beneath the wing of night;
There is an Ear that never shuts
   When sink the beams of light.

There is an Arm that never tires
   When human strength gives way;
There is a Love that never fails
   When earthly loves decay.

That Eye is fix'd on seraph throngs:
That Ear is fill'd with angel's songs;
That Arm upholds the worlds on high;
That Love is thron'd beyond the sky.   *Heber.*

God moves in a mysterious way
   His wonders to perform;
He plants His footsteps in the sea,
   And rides upon the storm.   *Cowper.*

All things that are on earth shall wholly pass away.
Except the love of God, which shall live and last for aye.
                                Bryant.

How calmly may we commit ourselves to the hands of Him
who bears up the world—of Him who has created, and who provides for the joy even of insects, as carefully as if He were their
Father!   *Richter.*

'Tis hard to find God, but to comprehend Him, as He is,
is labor without end.   *Herrick.*

At whose sight all the stars
Hide their diminish'd heads.   *Milton.*

GOLD.

   The picklock,
That never fails.   *Massinger.*

O cursed lust of gold! when for thy sake
The fool throws up his interest in both worlds
First starved in this, then damn'd in that to come.   *Blair.*

O, what a world of vile ill-favor'd faults
Look handsome in three hundred pounds a year.

Shakespeare.

'Tis gold so pure
It cannot bear the stamp without alloy. *Dryden.*

GOOD.

That which is good to be done, cannot be done too soon; and if it is neglected to be done early, it will frequently happen that it will not be done at all. *Bishop Mant.*

Hard was their lodging, homely was their food
For all their luxury was doing good. *Garth.*

Good, the more
Communicated, more abundant grows. *Milton.*

GOOD BREEDING.

Virtue itself often offends when coupled with bad manners.

Middleton.

Good breeding shows itself most where, to an ordinary eye, it appears the least. *Addison.*

One principal object of good-breeding is to suit our behavior to the three several degrees of men.—our superiors, our equals, and those below us. *Swift.*

A man's good-breeding is the best security against another's bad manners. *Chesterfield.*

The scholar without good-breeding is a pedant, the philosopher a cynic, the soldier a brute, and every man disagreeable.

Chesterfield.

GOOD-HUMOR.

Good humor is the health of the soul sadness its poison.

Stanislaus.

GOOD-NATURE.

That inexhaustible good nature, which is itself the most precious gift of Heaven, spreading itself like oil over the troubled sea of thought, and keeping the mind smooth and equable in the roughest weather.   *Irving.*

GOODNESS.

Goodness is beauty in its best estate.   *Marlowe.*

Kind hearts are more than coronets,
And simple faith than Norman blood.   *Tennyson.*

He has more goodness in his little finger
Than you have in your whole body.   *Swift.*

GOOD-NIGHT.

To all, to each, a fair good night,
And pleasing dreams, and slumbers light.   *Scott.*

GOSSIP.

For my part I can compare her to nothing but the sun; for, like him, she takes no rest, nor ever sets in one place but to rise in another.   *Dryden.*

GOVERNING.

A man must first govern himself ere he be fit to govern a family, and his family ere he fit to bear the government in the commonwealth.   *Sir Walter Raleigh.*

GOVERNMENT.

It is better for a city to be governed by a good man than by good laws.   *Aristotle.*

They that govern most make the least noise. You see, when they row in a barge, they that do drudgery work, slash and puff, and sweat, but he that governs sits quietly at the stern, and is scarce seen to stir.   *Selden.*

For forms of government let fools contest;
Whate'er is best administer'd is best. *Pope.*

We are more heavily taxed by our idleness, pride and folly than we are taxed by government. *Franklin.*

GRACE.

Some hae meat that canna eat,
  And some would eat that want it;
But we hae meat, and we can eat,
  Sae let the Lord be thankit. *Burns.*

GRATITUDE.

  To the generous mind
The heaviest debt is that of gratitude,
When 'tis not in our power to repay it.
  Dr. Thomas Franklin.

The debt immense of endless gratitude. *Milton.*

What is grandeur, what is power?
Heavier toil, superior pain!
What the bright reward we gain?
The grateful mem'ry of the good.
Sweet is the breath of vernal shower,
The bee's collected treasure sweet,
Sweet music's melting fall, but sweeter yet
The still small voice of gratitude. *Gray.*

He who receives a good turn should never forget it; he who does one should never remember it. *Charron.*

GRAVE.

  The reconciling grave
Swallows distinction first, that made us foes:
There all lie down in peace together. *Southern.*

There the wicked cease from troubling; and the weary be at rest. There the prisoners rest together; they hear not the voice of the oppressor. The small and great are there; and the

115

servant is free from his master. *Job* iii, 17, 18.

A grave, wherever found, preaches a short and pithy sermon of the soul. *Hawthorne.*

GRAVE-DIGGER.

The houses that he makes last till doomsday.

Shakespeare.

GRAVITY.

Gravity is a mystery of the body, invented to conceal the defects of the mind. *La Rochefoucauld.*

Too much gravity argues a shallow mind. *Lavater.*

GREATNESS.

He doth bestride the narrow world,
Like a Colossus; and we petty men
Walk under his huge legs, and peep about
To find ourselves dishonorable graves. *Shakespeare.*

In my stars I am above thee, but be not afraid of greatness; some are born great, some achieve greatness, and some have greatness thrust upon them. *Shakespeare.*

Oh! greatness! thou art a flattering dream,
A wat'ry bubble, lighter than the air. *Tracy.*

Lives of great men all remind us
    We can make our lives sublime,
And departing leave behind us
    Footprints on the sands of time;
Footprints that perhaps another,
    Sailing o'er life's solemn main,
A forlorn and shipwreck'd brother,
    Seeing, shall take heart again. *Longfellow.*

What millions died that Caesar might be great! *Campbell.*

The greatest truths are the simplest: so are the greatest men.

GRIEF.

And but he's something stain'd
With grief, that's beauty's canker, thou might'st call him
A goodly person.   *Shakespeare.*

What a rich feast the canker grief has made;
How has it suck'd the roses of thy cheeks!
And drunk the liquid crystal of thy eyes.   *Sewell.*

Oh! grief hath chang'd me since you saw me last;
And careful hours, with time's deform'd hand,
Have written strange defeatures in my face.   *Shakespeare.*

Excess of grief for the deceased is madness; for it is an injury to the living, and the dead know it not.   *Xenophon.*

What's gone, and what's past help
Should be past grief.   *Shakespeare*

'Tis impotent to grieve for what is past,
And unavailing to exclaim.   *Harvard.*

A malady
Preys on my heart, that medicine cannot reach
Invisible and cureless.   *Maturin.*

Grief, madam! 'Tis the pensiveness of joy,
Too deep for language—too serene for mirth.   *Talfourd.*

Grief knits two hearts in closer bonds than happiness ever
can; and common sufferings are far stronger links than common
joys.   *Lamartine.*

The storm of grief bears hard upon his youth,
And bends him like a drooping flower to earth.   *Rowe.*

Thine is a grief that wastes the heart,
    Like mildew on a tulip's dyes,—
When hope, deferr'd but to depart,
    Loses its smiles but keeps its sighs.   *L. E. Landon.*

GRUDGE.

If I can catch him once upon the hip
I will feed fat the ancient grudge I bear him.

Shakespeare.

GRUMBLING.

Everyone must see daily, instances of people who complain from a mere habit of complaining.   *Anon.*

GUARD.

It is better to be always upon your guard, than to suffer once.   *Latin Proverb.*

GUEST.

A pretty woman is a welcome guest.   *Byron.*

Unbidden guests
Are often welcomest when they are gone.   *Shakespeare.*

GUILT.

He swears, but he is sick at heart;
    He laughs, but he turns deadly pale;
His restless eye and sudden start—
    These tell the dreadful tale
That will be told: it needs no words from thee
Thou self-sold slave to guilt and misery.   *Dana.*

From the body of one guilty deed
A thousand ghostly fears and haunting thoughts prcceed.
                    Wordsworth.

So full of artless jealousy is guilt
It spills itself in fearing to be spilt.   *Shakespeare.*

And oh! that pang where more that madness lies,
The worm that will not sleep, and never dies.   *Byron.*

    God hath yok'd to guilt
Her pale tormentor—misery.   *Bryant.*

HABIT.

Habit gives endurance, and fatigue is the best nightcap.
                    Kincaid.

The chain of habit coils itself around the heart like a serpent, to gnaw and stifle it. *Hazlitt.*

A new cask will long preserve the tincture of the liquor with which it was first impregnated. *Horace.*

HABITS.

All habits gather by unseen degrees
As brooks make rivers, rivers run to seas. *Dryden.*

The diminutive chains of habit are seldom heavy enough to be felt until they are too strong to be broken. *Johnson.*

Small habits well pursued, betimes,
May reach the dignity of crimes. *Hannah More.*

HAPPINESS.

The sweetest bird builds near the ground,
   The loveliest flower springs low;
And we must stoop for happiness
   If we its worth would know. *Swain.*

That something still . . .
For which we bear to live or dare to die. *Pope.*

How cheap
Is genuine happiness, and yet how dearly
Do we all pay for its base counterfeit!
We fancy wants, which to supply, we dare
Danger and death, enduring the privation
Of all free nature offers in her bounty,
To attain that which, in its full fruition,
Brings but satiety. The poorest man
May taste of nature in her element;
Pure, wholesome, never cloying; while the richest,
From the same stores, does but elaborate
A pungent dish of well-concocted poison. *J. N. Barker.*

I earn what I eat, get what I wear, owe no man hate, envy no man's happiness, glad of other men's good, content with my harm. *Shakespeare.*

Know then this truth, enough for man to know
Virtue alone is happiness below.   *Pope.*

Our happiness in this world depends on the affections we
are enabled to inspire.   *Duchesse de Praslin.*

What nothing earthly gives, or can destroy
The soul's calm sunshine and the heartfelt joy.   *Pope.*

Perfect happiness, I believe, was never intended by the
Deity to be the lot of one of His creatures in this world; but
that He has very much put in our power the nearness of our
approaches to it, is what I have steadfastly believed. *Jefferson.*

Happiness is in the taste, and not in the things themselves;
we are happy from possessing what we like, not from possessing what others like.   *La Rochefoucauld.*

Surely happiness is reflective like the light of heaven; and
every countenance, bright with smiles and glowing with innocent enjoyment, is a mirror, transmitting to others the rays of
a supreme and ever-shining benevolence. *Washington Irving.*

After long storms and tempests overblown,
The sun at length his joyous face doth cleare;
So when fortune all her spight hath showne,
Some blissful houres at last must needs appeare.
Else should afflicted wights oft-times despeare.   *Spenser.*

If solid happiness we prize,
Within our breast this jewel lies,
And they are fools who roam;
The world has nothing to bestow;
From our own selves our joys must flow
And that dear hut—our home.   *Cotton.*

        All who joy would win
Must share it—happiness was born a twin.   *Byron.*

HAPPINESS AND WISDOM.

There is the difference between happiness and wisdom; he
that thinks himself the happiest man really is so; but he that
thinks himself the wisest, is generally the greatest fool. *Colton.*

HARLOT.

She weaves the winding-sheets of souls, and lays
Them in the urn of everlasting death.   *Pollok.*

    'Tis the strumpet's plague
To beguile many, and be beguiled by one.   *Shaftesbury.*

HARVEST.

    Glowing scene!
Nature's long holiday! luxuriant—rich
In her proud progeny, she smiling marks
Their graces, now mature, and wonder fraught!
Hail! season exquisite!—and hail ye sons
Of rural toil!—ye blooming daughters ye
Who, in the lap of hardy labor rear'd,
Enjoy the mind unspotted.   *Mary Robinson.*

HASTE.

Running together all about,
The servants put each other out,
Till the grave master had decreed,
The more haste, ever the worst speed.   *Churchill.*

HATRED.

A man should not allow himself to hate even his enemies,
because if you indulge this passion, on some occasions, it will
rise of itself in others: if you hate your enemies, you will con-
tract such a vicious habit of mind, as by degrees will break out
upon those who are your friends, or those who are indifferent
to you.   *Plutarch.*

Thou mayst hold a serpent by the tongue,
A chafed lion by the mortal paw,
A fasting tiger safer by the tooth,
Than keep in peace that hand which thou dost hold.

                            Shakespeare.

It is the nature of the human disposition to hate him whom
you have injured.   *Tacitus.*

Now hatred is by far the longest pleasure;
Men love in haste, but they detest at leisure.   *Byron.*

HEALTH.

He who has health has hope, and he who has hope has
everything.   *Arabian Proverb.*

People who are always taking care of their health are like
misers, who are hoarding a treasure which they have never spirit
enough to enjoy.   *Sterne.*

The only way for a rich man to be healthy is, by exercise
and abstinence, to live as if he were poor.   *Sir W. Temple*

The common ingredients of health and long life are:
Great temp'rance, open air,
Easy labor, little care.   *Sir P. Sidney.*

For life is not to live, but to be well.   *Martial.*

Be sober and temperate, and you will be healthy.
                                              B. Franklin.

The surest road to health, say what they will,
Is never to suppose we shall be ill.   *Churchill.*

HEART.

Heaven's Sovereign spares all beings but himself,
That hideous sight—a naked human heart.   *Young.*

The honest heart that's free frae a
    Intended fraud or guile,
However fortune kick the ba'
    Has aye some cause to smile.   *Burns.*

A young maiden's heart
Is a rich soil, wherein lie many germs
Hid by the cunning hand of nature there
To put forth blossoms in their fittest season;
And though the love of home first breaks the soil,
With its embracing tendrils clasping it,
Other affections, strong and warm will grow
While that one fades, as summer's flush of bloom

122

Succeed the gentle budding of the spring.

Mrs. F. Kemble Butler.

The heart aye's the part aye
That makes us right or wrang. *Burns.*

I have ease and I have health,
  And I have spirits light as air;
And more than wisdom, more than wealth—
  A merry heart that laughs at care. *H. H. Milman.*

The human heart is often the victim of the sensations of
the moment; success intoxicates it to presumption, and disap-
poin ment dejects and terrifies it. *Volney.*

A recent moralist has affirmed that the human heart is like
a jug. No mortal can look into its recesses, and you can only
judge of its purity by what comes out of it. *Anon.*

HEAVEN.

Heaven is above all yet; there sits a judge
That no king can corrupt. *Shakespeare.*

Heaven's gates are not so highly arch'd
As princes' palaces; they that enter there
Must go upon their knees. *Webster.*

By heaven we understand a state of happiness infinite in
degree, and endless in duration. *Franklin.*

Eye hath not seen it, my gentle boy;
Ear hath not heard its deep song of joy;
Dreams cannot picture a world so fair;
Sorrow and death may not enter there;
Time doth not breathe on its fadeless bloom
For beyond the clouds, and beyond the tomb,
  It is there, it is there, my child. *Mrs. Hemans.*

A Persian's heaven is easily made,
'Tis but black eyes and lemonade. *Moore.*

HEAVEN AND EARTH.

Heaven—it is God's throne. The earth—it is his footstool.
Matthew v., 34.

HELL.

Hell is truth seen too late.   *H. G. Adams.*

Divines and dying men may talk of Hell
But in my heart her several torments dwell.   *Shakespeare.*

Hell has no limits, nor is circumscribed
In one self place; but where we are in hell
And where hell is, there must we ever be
And to be short, when all the world dissolves,
And every creature shall be purified,
All places shall be hell that are not heaven.   *Marlowe.*

HERO.

Whoever, with an earnest soul,
   Strives for some end from this low world afar,
Still upward travels though he miss the goal,
   And strays—but towards a star.   *Bulwer.*

     All may be heroes:—
"The man who rules his spirit," saith the voice
Which cannot err,—"is greater than the man
Who takes a city." Hence it surely follows,
If each man would govern wisely, and thus show
Truth, courage, knowledge, power, benevolence
All, all the princely soul of private virtues,
Then each would be a prince, a hero—greater—
He will be a man in likeness of his maker!   *Mrs. Hale.*

HEROISM.

Heroism—the divine relation which in all times unites a
great man to other men.   *Carlyle.*

HIGHWAYMAN.

Gentlemen of the shade, minions of the moon.

Shakespeare.

HISTORY.

Her ample page
Rich with the spoils of time.   *Gray.*

Some are to be read, some to be studied, and some may be neglected entirely, not only without detriment, but with advantage.   *Bolingbroke.*

Some write a narrative of wars and feats,
Of heroes little known, and call the rant
A history; describe the man of whom
His own coevals took but little note,
And paint his person, character, and views,
As they had known him from his mother's womb.

Cowper.

What are most of the histories of the world, but lies? Lies immortalized and consigned over as a perpetual abuse and a flaw upon prosperity.   *South.*

HOLINESS.

Blessed is the memory of those who have kept themselves unspotted *from* the world! Yet more blessed and more dear the memory of those who have kept themselves unspotted in the world.   ·   *Mrs. Jameson.*

HOME.

Bare walls make a gadding housewife.   *Fielding.*

The paternal hearth, that rallying place of the affections.
Washington Irving.

His warm but simple home where he enjoys
With her who shares his pleasures and his heart
Sweet converse.   *Cowper.*

Mid pleasures and palaces though we may roam,
Be it ever so humble there's no place like home.
J. Howard Payne.

Home is the sacred refuge of our life,
Secured from all approaches but a wife;

If thence we fly, the cause admits no doubt,
None but an inmate foe could force us out.   *Dryden.*

HONESTY.

Honesty coupled to beauty, is to have honey a sauce to
sugar.   *Shakespeare.*

What is becoming is honest, and whatever is honest must
be becoming.   *Cicero.*

Who is the honest man?
He that doth still and strongly good pursue,
To God, his neighbor, and himself most true:
Whom neither force nor fawning can
Unpin, or wrench from giving all their due.   *Herbert.*

Let honesty be as the breath of thy soul, and never forget
to have a penny, when all thy expenses are enumerated and
paid; then shall thou reach the point of happiness, and inde-
pendence shall be thy shield and buckler, thy helmet and crown;
then shall thy soul walk upright, nor stoop to the silken wretch
because he hath riches, nor pocket an abuse, because the hand
which offers it wears a ring set with diamonds.   *Franklin.*

Lands mortgag'd may return, and more esteem'd,
But honesty once pawn'd, is ne'er redeem'd.   *Middleton.*

The maxim that "Honesty is the best policy" is one which,
perhaps, no one is ever habitually guided by in practice. An
honest man is always before it, and a knave is generally behind it.   *Whately.*

A wit's a feather, and a chief's a rod;
An honest man's the nobles work of God.   *Pope.*

Heav'n that made me honest, made me more
Than ever king did when he made a lord.   *Rowe.*

To be honest, as this world goes,
Is to be one pick'd out of ten thousand.   *Shakespeare.*

The more honesty a man has, the less he affects the air of
a saint.   *Lavater.*

HONOR.

Honor's a good brooch to wear in a man's hat at all times.
Jonson.

Honor is like that glassy bubble,
That finds philosophers such trouble,
Whose least part crack'd, the whole does fly
And wits are crack'd to find out why. *Butler.*

Honor and shame from no condition rise;
Act well your part; there all the honor lies. *Pope.*

Honor's a fine imaginary notion.
That draws in raw and unexperienced men
To real mischiefs, while they hunt a shadow. *Addison.*

No man of honor, as that word is usually understood, did ever pretend that his honor obliged him to be chaste and temperate, to pay his creditors, to be useful to his country, or to do good to mankind, to endeavor to be wise or learned, to regard his word his promise, or his oath. *Swift.*

The noblest spur unto the sons of fame,
Is thirst for honor. *John Hall.*

Our own heart, and not other men's opinions forms our true honor. *Coleridge.*

Better to die ten thousand deaths
Than wound my honor. *Addison.*

Woman's honor
Is nice as ermine,—'twill not bear a soil. *Dryden.*

HOPE.

It is best to hope only for things possible and probable; he that hopes too much shall deceive himself at last; especially if his industry does not go along with his hopes; for hope without action is a barren undoer. *Feltham.*

Hope
Is such a bait, it covers any hook. *Jonson.*

Come then, oh care! oh grief! oh woe!

Oh troubles! mighty in your kind,
I have a balm ye ne'er can know,
   A hopeful mind.   *F. Vane.*

Auspicious hope in thy sweet garden grow
Wreaths for each toil, a charm for every woe.   *Campbell.*

All, all forsook the friendless guilty mind,
But hope, the charmer, linger'd still behind.   *Campbell.*

Hope deferred maketh the heart sick.   *Prov.* xiii, 12.

Hope is the pillar that holds up the world.
Hope is the dream of a waking man.   *Pliny.*

—Hopes that beckon with delusive gleams,
Till the eye dances in the void of dreams.   *Holmes.*

Hope springs eternal in the human breast,
Man never is, but always to be blest.   *Pope.*

Hope is a flatterer, but the most upright of parasites; for she frequents the poor man's hut, as well as the palace of his superior.   *Shenstone.*

Hope, of all passions, most befriends us here.   *Young.*

Our greatest good, and what we least can spare,
Is hope; the last of all our evils, fear.   *Armstrong.*

Hope is like the cork to the net, which keeps the soul from sinking in despair; and fear is like the lead to the net, which keeps it from floating in presumption.   *Watson.*

The setting of a great hope is like the setting of the sun. The brightness of our life is gone, shadows of the evening fall around us, and the world seems but a dim reflection itself—a broader shadow. We look forward into the coming lonely night; the soul withdraws itself. Then stars arise, and the night is wholly.   *Longfellow.*

He that loses hope may part with anything.   *Congreve.*

Where no hope is left, is left no fear.   *Milton.*

Hope! fortune's cheating lottery
Where for one prize a thousand blanks there are.   *Cowley.*

The mighty hopes that make us men.   *Tennyson.*

However deceitful hope may be, yet she carries us on pleasantly to the end of life.   *La Rochefoucauld.*

A propensity to hope and joy is real riches; one to fear and sorrow real poverty.   *Hume.*

True hope is swift and flies with swallow's wings;
Kings it makes gods, and meaner creatures kings.

          Shakespeare.

Hope is the fawning traitor of the mind,
Which, while it cozens with a color'd friendship
Robs us of our best virtue—resolution.   *Lee.*

HOSPITALITY.

Hospitality to the better sort, and charity to the poor; two virtues that are never exercised so well as when they accompany each other.   *Atterbury.*

Hours are golden links;—God's tokens reaching heaven.

          Dickens.

Catch, then, oh! catch the transient hour,
    Improve each moment as it flies;
Life's a short summer—man a flower;
    He dies—alas! how soon he dies.   *Johnson.*

HOUSE.

A house is never perfectly furnished for enjoyment, unless there is a child in it rising three years old, and a kitten rising six weeks.   *Southey.*

My precept to all who build is, that the owner should be an ornament to the house, and not the house to the owner.

          Cicero.

Nothing lovelier can be found
In woman, than to study household good,
And good works in her husband to promote.   *Milton.*

HUMAN NATURE.

If we did not take great pains, and were not at great expense to corrupt our nature, our nature would never corrupt us.
Lord Clarendon.

Our humanity were a poor thing were it not for the divinity which stirs within us.
Bacon.

HUMILITY.

Highest when it stoops
Lowest before the holy throne; throws down
Its crown abased; forgets itself, admires,
And breathes ador'ing praise.
Pollok.

Humility, that low sweet root,
From which all heavenly virtues shoot.
Moore.

The sufficiency of my merit is to know that my merit is not sufficient.
Augustine.

Humility is a virtue all preach, none practice, and yet everybody is content to hear. The master thinks it good doctrine for his servant, the laity for the clergy, and the clergy for the laity.
Selden.

Be wise,
Soar not too high to fall, but stoop to rise.
Massinger.

My endeavors
Have ever come too short of my desire
Shakespeare.

HUMOR.

Let your humor always be good humor in both senses. If it comes of a bad humor, it is pretty sure not to belie its parentage.
Anon.

Some things are of that nature as to make
One's fancy chuckle while his heart doth ache.
Bunyan.

HUNGER.

Famish'd people must be slowly nursed,
And fed by spoonfuls, else they always burst.
Byron.

Hunger is the best seasoning for meat, and thirst for drink. *Cicero.*

HYPOCRISY.

O serpent heart, hid with flow'ring face!
Did ever dragon keep so fair a cave? *Shakespeare.*

Obey me, features, for one supple moment:
You shall not long be tortured. Here in courts
We must not wear the soldier's honest face. *H. Thompson.*

Trust not those cunning waters of his eyes,
For villainy is not without much rheum;
And he long-traded in it, makes it seem
Like rivers of remorse and innocence. *Shakespeare.*

Thy very looks are lies; eternal falsehood
Smiles in thy lips, and flatters in thine eye. *Smith.*

The devil can cite Scripture for his pupose.
An evil soul, producing holy witness,
Is like a villian with a smiling cheek;
A goodly apple rotten at the heart;
Oh, what a goodly outside falsehood hath! *Shakespeare.*

Hypocrisy is the homage which vice pays to virtue.
La Rochefoucauld.

HYPOCRITE.

The fawning, sneaking, and flattering hypocrite, that will do, or be anything, for his own advantage. *Stillingfleet.*

Hypocrites do the devil's drudgery in Christ's livery.
Matthew Henry.

IDEA.

An idea, like a ghost, (according to the common notion of ghost,) must be spoken to a little before it will explain itself.
Dickens.

He doth nothing but talk of his horse; and he makes it a

great appropriation to his own good parts, that he can shoe him
himself. *Shakespeare.*

IDLENESS.

Absence of occupation is not rest
A mind quite vacant is a mind distress'd. *Cowper.*

Evil thoughts intrude in an unemployed mind, as natural-
ly as worms are generated in a stagnant pool. *From the Latin.*

Sluggish idleness—the nurse of sin. *Spenser.*

Idleness travels very slowly, and poverty soon overtakes
her. *Hunter.*

IDOLATRY.

'Tis mad idolatry,
To make the service greater than the god. *Shakespeare.*

IF.

Your If is the only peace-maker,—
Much virtue in If. *Shakespeare.*

IGNORANCE.

Where ignorance is bliss
'Tis folly to be wise. *Gray.*

I hardly know so true a mark of a little mind as the servile
imitation of another. *Greville.*

It is impossible to make people understand their ignorance,
for it requires knowledge to perceive it; and, therefore, he that
can perceive it hath it not. *Jeremy Taylor.*

ILLS.

Common and vulgar people ascribe all ill that they feel, to
others; people of little wisdom ascribe to themselves; people
of much wisdom, to no one. *Epictetus.*

Keep what you've got; the ills that we know are the best.

Plautus.

ILLUSION.

Some there be that shadows kiss;
Some have but a shadow's bliss.

Shakespeare.

IMAGINATION.

The beings of the mind are not of clay;
Essentially immortal, they create
And multiply in us a brighter ray
And more beloved existence.

Byron.

IMITATION.

A good imitation is the most perfect *originality.*   *Voltaire.*

Men are so constituted that everybody undertakes what he
sees another successful in, whether he has aptitude for it or not.

Goethe.

IMMODESTY.

Immodest words admit of no defence
For want of decency is want of sense.

Pope.

IMMORTALITY.

Immortality o'ersweeps
All pains, all tears, all time, all fears—and peals,
Like the eternal thunders of the deep,
Into my ears this truth—Thou liv'st for ever.

Anon.

Love, which proclaims thee human bids thee know
A truth more lofty in thy lowliest hour
Than shallow glory taught to human power,
"What's human is immortal!"

Bulwer.

IMPATIENCE.

Impatience dries the blood sooner than age or sorrow.

Creon.

IMPLACABILITY.

There's no more mercy in him than there is milk in a male tiger.   *Shakespeare.*

IMPOSSIBLE.

Impossible is a word only to be found in the dictionary of fools.   *Napoleon I.*

IMPRESSIONS.

The mind unlearns with difficulty what it has long learned.
                                        Seneca.

IMPUDENCE.

The way to avoid the imputation of impudence is not to be ashamed of what we do, but never to do what we ought to be ashamed of.   *Tully.*

What! canst thou say all this and never blush?
                                        Shakespeare.

IMPULSE.

Act upon your impulses, but pray that they may be directed by God.   *Emerson Tennent.*

Since the generality of persons act from impulse much more than from principle, men are neither so good nor so bad as we are apt to think them.   *Hare.*

INACTION.

Or doing nothing with a deal of skill.   *Cowper.*

It is better to have nothing to do, than to be doing nothing.
                                        Attilus.

INCIVILITY.

A man has no more right to say an uncivil thing, than to act one; no more right to say a rude thing to another, than to knock him down.   *Johnson.*

INCONSTANCY.

The dream on the pillow,
  That flits with the day,
The leaf of the willow
  A breath bears away;
The dust on the blossom,
  The spray of the sea;
Ay,—ask thine own bosom—
  Are emblems of thee.   *L. E. Landon.*

          O heaven! Were man
But constant, he were perfect: that one error
Fills him with faults; make him run through sins:
Inconstancy falls off ere it begins.   *Shakespeare.*

INDEPENDENCE.

Bow to no patron's insolence; rely
On no frail hopes, in freedom live and die.   *Seneca.*

Slave to no sect, who takes no private road
But looks through nature up to nature's God.   *Pope.*

INDUSTRY.

Sloth makes all things difficult, but industry all easy; and he that riseth late, must trot all day, and shall scarce overtake his business at night; while laziness travels so slowly, that poverty soon overtakes him.   *Franklin.*

It sweeteneth our enjoyments, and seasoneth our attainments with a delightful relish.   *Barrow.*

At the working-man's house hunger looks in, but dares not enter! nor will the bailiff or the constable enter; for industry pays debts, but despair increaseth them. *Franklin.*

INEXPERIENCE.

He jests at scars who never felt a wound. *Shakespeare.*

INFANCY.

Heaven lies about us in our infancy. *Wordsworth.*

INFANT.

Or as the plumage of an angel's wing
    Where every tint of rainbow beauty blends.

Mrs. Welby.

Ere sin could blight, or sorrow fade,
    Death came with friendly care;
The opening bud to heav'n convey'd,
    And bade it blossom there. *Coleridge.*

    He smiles and sleeps! sleep on
And smile, thou little young inheritor
Of a world scarce less young; sleep on and smile!
Thine are the hours and days when both are cheering.
And innocent. *Byron.*

INFIDELITY.

When once infidelity can persuade men that they shall
die like beasts, they will soon be brought to *live like beasts* also.
South.

INFLUENCE.

Not one false man but does unaccountable mischief.

Carlyle.

As a little silvery circular ripple, set in motion by the falling pebble, expands from its inch of radius to the whole compass of a pool, so there is not a child—not an infant Moses—
placed, however softly, in his bulrush ark upon the sea of time,

whose existence does not stir a ripple, gyrating outward and on, until it shall have moved across and spanned the whole ocean of God's eternity, stirring even the river of life, and the fountains at which the angels drink.   *Elihu Burritt.*

INGRATITUDE.

I hate ingratitude more in a man,
Than lying, vainness, babbling, drunkenness
Or any taint of vice, whose strong corruption
Inhabits our frail blood.   *Shakespeare.*

Blow, blow, thou winter wind,
Thou art not so unkind
  As man's ingratitude;
Thy tooth is not so keen,
Because thou art not seen,
  Although thy breath be rude.   *Shakespeare.*

INJURIES.

A man should be careful never to tell tales of himself to his own disadvantage; people may be amused, and laugh at the time, but they will be remembered, and brought up against him upon some subsequent occasion.   *Johnson.*

INNOCENCE.

O innocence, the sacred amulet,
'Gainst all the poisons of infirmity,
Of all misfortunes, injury and death!   *Chapman.*

Against the head which innocence secures,
Insidious malice aims her dart in vain;
Turn'd backwards by the powerful breath of heav'n.

                                               Johnson.

There is no courage, but in innocence,
No constancy, but in an honest cause.   *Southern.*

O that I had my innocence again!
My untouch'd honor! But I wish in vain.
The fleece that has been by the dyer stain'd
Never again its native whiteness gain'd.   *Waller.*

They that know no evil will suspect none. *Ben Jonson.*

Innocence is always unsuspicious. *Haliburton.*

INSTINCT.

In the nice bee what sense so subtly true
From pois'nous herbs extract the healing dew? *Pope.*

By a divine instinct, men's minds distrust
Ensuing danger; as by proof we see
The waters swell before a boisterous storm. *Shakespeare.*

INSULT.

Of all the griefs that harass the distress'd,
Sure the most bitter is a scornful jest;
Fate never wounds more deep the generous heart,
Than when a blockhead's insult points the dart.

Dr. Johnson.

INTELLECT.

The intellect of the wise is like glass; it admits the light of heaven and reflects it. *Hare.*

INTENTIONS.

A man who is always forgetting his best intentions, may be said to be a thoroughfare of good resolutions. *Mrs. Jameson.*

INTRUSIVENESS.

The great secret of life is never to be in the way of others.
Haliburton.

IRRESOLUTION.

I hope when you know the worst you will at once leap into the river and swim through handsomely, and not, weather-beaten by the divers blasts of irresolution, stand shivering upon the brink. *Suckling.*

138

IVY.

As creeping ivy clings to wood or stone
And hides the ruin that it feeds upon.   *Cowper.*

JEALOUSY.

    Trifles light as air
Are to the jealous, confirmations strong
As proofs of holy writ.   *Shakespeare.*

    Beware of jealousy,
It is the green-eyed monster which doth mock
The meat it feeds on.   *Shakespeare.*

Yet there is one more cursed than them all,
That canker-worm, that monster, jealousy,
Which eats the heart and feeds upon the gall,
Turning all love's delight to misery,
Through fear of losing his felicity.
Ah, gods! that ever ye that monster placed
In gentle love, that all his joys defaced!   *Spenser*

The venom clamors of a jealous woman
Poison more deadly than a mad dog's tooth.   *Shakespeare.*

JEST.

A jest's prosperity lies in the ear
Of him that hears it, never in the tongue
Of him who makes it.   *Shakespeare.*

JESTS.

Laughter should dimple the cheek, not furrow the brow. A jest should be such, that all shall be able to join in the laugh which it occasions; but if it bear hard upon one of the company, like the crack of a string, it makes a stop in the music.   *Feltham.*

JOLLITY.

Give me health and a day, and I will make ridiculous the pomp of emperors.   *Emerson.*

JOURNALISM.

A journalist is a grumbler, a censurer, a giver of advice, a regent of sovereigns, a tutor of nations. Four hostile newspapers are more to be feared than a thousand bayonets.   *Napoleon I.*

JOY.

Joy descends gently upon us like the evening dew, and does not patter down like a hail-storm.   *Richter.*

We show our present joking, giggling race,
True joy consists in gravity and grace.   *Garrick.*

How much better it is to weep at joy than to joy at weeping.
Shakespeare.

JOYS.

Little joys refresh us constantly, like house-bread, and never bring disgust; and great ones, like sugar-bread, briefly, and then bring it.   *Richter.*

JUDGE.

He softens the hard rigor of the laws,
Blunts their keen edge, and grinds their harpy claws.
Garth.

Four things belong to a judge; to hear courteously, to answer wisely, to consider soberly, and to decide impartially.
Socrates.

JUDGING.

Forbear to judge, for we are sinners all.   *Shakespeare.*

'Tis better that a man's own works, than that another man's words should praise him.   *L'Estrange.*

Every one complains of the badness of his memory, but nobody of his judgment.   *La Rochefoucauld.*

140

You think it is a want of judgment that he changes his opinion. Do you think it a proof that your scales are bad because they vibrate with every additional weight that is added to either side? *Edgeworth.*

JUSTICE.

Justice like lightning, ever should appear
To few men's ruin, but to all men's fear.　　*Swetnam.*

1.　Do you know me, Mr. Justice?
2.　Justice is blind; he knows nobody.　　*Dryden.*

Justice is lame as well as blind among us.　　*Otway.*

　　　　　Be just and fear not;
Let all the ends thou aim'st at be thy country's,
Thy God's, and truth's.　　*Shakespeare.*

KICK.

A kick, that scarce would move a horse
May kill a sound divine.　　*Cowper.*

KIND.

One touch of nature makes the whole world kin.
　　　　　　　　　　　　Shakespeare.

KINDNESS.

That best portion of a good man's life
His little nameless, unremembered acts of kindness and of
　love.　　　　　　　　　*Wordsworth.*

The drying up a single tear has more
Of honest fame, than shedding seas of gore.　　*Byron.*

KING.

A crown
Golden in show, is but a wreath of thorns;

Brings danger, troubles, cares, and sleepless nights
To him who wears a regal diadem.   *Milton.*

Then happy low, lie down!
Uneasy lies the head that wears a crown.   *Shakespeare.*

A king that would not feel his crown too heavy for him,
must wear it every day; but if he thinks it too light, he knoweth
not of what metal it is made.   *Bacon.*

KISS.

Soft child of love—thou balmy bliss,
Inform me, O delicious kiss!
Why thou so suddenly art gone
Lost in the moment thou art won.   *Dr. Wolcot.*

I came to feel how far above
All fancy, pride, and fickle maidenhood
All earthly pleasure, all imagined good
Was the warm tremble of a devout kiss.   *Keats.*

My lips pressed themselves involuntarily to hers—a long,
long kiss, burning intense—concentrating emotion, heart, soul, all
the rays of life's light, into a single focus.   *Bulwer.*

Sweet were his kisses on my balmy lips,
As are the breezes breath'd amidst the groves
Of ripening spices on the height of day.   *Behn.*

Kiss the tear from her lip, you'll find the rose
The sweeter for the dew.   *Webster.*

KISSING.

Then kiss'd me hard;
As if he pluck'd up kisses by the roots,
That grew upon my lips.   *Shakespeare.*

A pleasing trembling thrills through all my blood
Whene'er you touch me with your melting hand;
But when you kiss, oh! 'tis not to be spoke.   *Gildon.*

142

KNAVE.

What a pestilent knave is this same! *Shakespeare.*

A beetle-headed flat-ear'd knave. *Shakespeare.*

A slippery and subtle knave; a finder out of occasions; that has an eye can stamp and counterfeit advantages, though true advantage never presents itself; a devilish knave. *Shakespeare.*

KNOWLEDGE.

The first step to knowledge is to know that we are ignorant.
Cecil.

Knowledge is power. *Bacon.*

The desire of knowledge, like the thirst of riches, increases ever with the acquisition of it. *Sterne.*

The profoundly wise do not declaim against superficial knowledge in others, as much as the profoundly ignorant.
Colton.

He that sips of many arts, drinks of none. *Fuller.*

The shortest and surest way of arriving at real knowledge is to unlearn the lessons we have been taught, to remount first principles, and to take nobody's word about them.
Bolingbroke.

KNOWLEDGE OF SELF.

The most difficult thing in life is to know yourself. *Thales.*

Man know thyself! All wisdom centers there. *Young.*

LABOR.

It is only by labor that thought can be made healthy, and only by thought that labor can be made happy; and the two cannot be separated with impunity. *Ruskin.*

Where love is there is no labor; and if there be labor, that labor is loved. *Austin.*

Numbering sands and drinking oceans dry.   *Shakespeare.*

You may as well go about to turn the sun to ice, by fanning in his face with a peacock's feather.   *Shakespeare.*

Letting down buckets into empty wells,
And growing old with drawing nothing up.   *Cowper.*

LANGUAGE.

Languages are the pedigrees of nations.   *Johnson.*

Language is fossil poetry.   *Anon.*

When nature's end of language is declined,
And men talk only to conceal the mind.   *Young.*

Speak the language of the company you are in; speak it purely, and unlarded with any other.   *Chesterfield.*

LARK.

Hark! how with lone and fluttering start
   The sky-lark soars above,
And with her full, melodious heart,
   She pours her strains of love.   *Mrs. Welby.*

LAUGHTER.

Madness, we fancy, gave an ill-timed birth
To grinning laughter and to frantic mirth.   *Prior.*

Man is the only creature endowed with the power of laughter; is he not the only one that deserves to be laughed at?
                                                        Greville.

How much lies in laughter; the cipher-*key* wherewith we decipher the whole man! some men wear an everlasting barren simper; in the smile of others lies the cold glitter, as of ice; the fewest are able to laugh what can be called laughing, but only sniff and titter and sniggle from the throat outwards, or at least produce some whiffling, husky cachinnation, as if they were laughing through wool; of none such comes good. The man who

144

cannot laugh is only fit for treasons, stratagems and spoils; but his own whole life is already a treason and a stratagem.

Carlyle.

The most utterly lost of all days, is that in which you have not once laughed. *Chamfort.*

LAW.

The good needs fear no law,
It is his safety, and the bad man's awe.

Massinger, Middleton and Rowley.

The English laws punish vice; the Chinese laws do more, they reward virtue. *Goldsmith.*

To go to law, is for two persons to kindle a fire at their own cost, to warm others, and singe themselves to cinders; and because they cannot agree, to what is truth and equity, they will both agree to unplume themselves, that others may be decorated with their feathers. *Feltham.*

LAWS.

When the state is most corrupt, then the laws are most multiplied. *Tacitus.*

Laws can discover sin, but not remove. *Milton.*

LAWYERS AND PHYSICIANS.

Commonly, physicians, like beer, are best when they are old, and lawyers, like bread, when they are young and new.

Fuller.

LEARNING.

A little learning is a dangerous thing! *Pope.*

Learning maketh young men temperate, is the comfort of old age, standing for wealth with poverty, and serving as an ornament to riches. *Cicero.*

LECTURE.

And every married man is certain
T'attend the lecture called the curtain.   *Lloyd.*

LEISURE.

I am never less at leisure than when at leisure, nor less
alone than when I am alone.   *Scipio Africanus.*

LENDING.

If you lend a person any money, it becomes lost for any
purposes of your own. When you ask for it back again, you
find a friend made an enemy by your own kindness. If you begin to press still further—either you must part with that which
you have intrusted, or else you must lose that friend. *Plautus.*

LETTERS.

Kind messages that pass from land to land,
    Kind letters that betray the heart's deep history,
In which we feel the pressure of a hand
    One touch of fire, and all the rest is mystery.

Longfellow.

Letters which are warmly sealed are often but coldly
opened.   *Richter.*

LIARS.

Past all shame—so past all truth.   *Shakespeare.*

They begin with making falsehood appear like truth, and
end with making truth itself appear like falsehood.

Shenstone.

LIBERTY.

Oh! liberty, thou goddess, heavenly bright,
Profuse of bliss, and pregnant with delight!   *Addison.*

146

Liberty! Liberty! how many crimes are committed in thy name.   *Madame Roland.*

    Oh! give me liberty,
For were ev'n Paradise my prison,
Still I should long to leap the crystal walls.   *Dryden.*

Liberty consists in the power of doing that which is permitted by law.   *Cicero.*

LIBRARIES.

Libraries are the shrines where all the relics of the ancient saints, full of true virtue, and that without delusion or imposture, are preserved and reposed.   *Bacon.*

LIE.

Sin has many tools, but a lie is the handle which fits them all.   *Holmes.*

He who tells a lie is not sensible how great a task he undertakes; for he must be forced to invent twenty more to maintain that one.   *Pope.*

LIFE.

Life is but a day at most.   *Burns.*

O life! thou art a galling load
Along a rough, a weary road.   *Burns.*

        My life is but a wind
Which passeth by, and leaves no print behind.   *Sandys.*

Life is as tedious as a twice told tale
Vexing the dull ear of a drowsy man.   *Shakespeare.*

At twenty years of age the will reigns; at thirty, the wit; and at forty, the judgment.   *Grattan.*

Our care should not be so much to live long, as to live well.   *Seneca.*

Life is real, life is earnest,

And the grave is not its goal;
Dust thou art, to dust returnest,
   Was not spoken of the soul.   *Longfellow.*

Like some fair hum'rists, life is most enjoy'd
When courted least; most worth, when disesteemed.
                            Young.

Life's but a walking shadow—a poor player,
That struts and frets his hour upon the stage,
And then is heard no more. It is a tale
Told by idiot, full of sound and fury
Signifying nothing.   *Shakespeare.*

Nor love thy life, nor hate; but whilst thou liv'st
Live well; how long, how short, permit to Heaven.
                            Milton.

That life is long which answers life's great end.   *Young.*

Live while you live the epicure would say
And seize the pleasures of the present day;
Live while you live the sacred preacher cries,
And give to God each moment as it flies.
Lord, in my views let both united be;
I live in pleasure when I live in thee.   *Philip Doddridge.*

To live long, it is necessary to live slowly.   *Cicero.*

Our life so fast away doth slide
   As doth an hungry eagle through the wind;
Or as a ship transported with the tide,
   Which in their passage leave no print behind.
                        Sir J. Davies.

The youngest in the morning are not sure
That till the night their life they can secure.
                        Sir J. Denham.

The vanity of human life is like a river, constantly passing
away, and yet constantly coming on.   *Pope.*

LIGHT.

The first creation of God in the works of the days was the

light of the sense, the last was the light of the reason; and his Sabbath work ever since is the illumination of the spirit.

Bacon.

Ethereal, first of things, quintessence, pure. *Milton.*

Is not light grander than fire? It is the same element in a state of purity. *Carlyle.*

And storied windows richly dight,
Casting a dim religious light. *Milton.*

LIGHT-FOOTEDNESS.

Pray you tread softly, that the blind mole may not.
Hear a footfall. *Shakespeare.*

LIGHT-HEARTEDNESS.

They pass best over the world who trip over it quickly; for it is but a bog—if we stop we sink. *Queen Elizabeth.*

A light heart lives long. *Shakespeare.*

LION.

A lion among ladies is a most fearful thing; for there is not a more fearful wild-fowl than your lion living. *Shakespeare.*

LIPS.

Her lips are roses over-washed with dew. *Greene.*

LISTENING.

Were we as eloquent as angels, yet should we please some men and some women much more by listening than by talking.
Colton.

LITERATURE.

Literature is the grindstone, to sharpen the coulters, and to whet their natural faculties. *Hammond.*

LIVING.

The man who will live above his present circumstances is in great danger of living in a little time much beneath them.

Addison.

From the time we first begin to know,
We live and learn, but not the wiser grow.   *Pomfret.*

He that spends all his life in sport is like one who wears nothing but fringes and eats nothing but sauces.   *Fuller.*

LOGIC.

It was a saying of the ancients, "Truth lies in a well;" and to carry on this metaphor, we may justly say that logic does supply us with steps, whereby we may go down to reach the water.   *Dr. I. Watts.*

LOGICIAN.

He was in logic a great critic,
Profoundly skilled in analytic;
He could distinguish and divide
A hair 'twixt south and southwest side
On either which he would dispute,
Confute, change hands, and still confute.   *Butler.*

LOQUACITY.

Learn to hold thy tongue. Five words cost Zacharias forty weeks' silence.   *Fuller.*

Gratiano speaks an infinite deal of nothing, more than any man in Venice; but his reasons are as two grains of wheat hid in two bushels of chaff; you seek all day ere you find them; and when you have them, they are not worth the search.

Shakespeare.

LOVE.

Love is the salt of life; a higher taste
It gives to pleasure, and then makes it last.   *Buckingham.*

The sweetest joy, the wildest woe is love;
The taint of earth, the odor of the skies is in it. *Bailey.*

Love is not altogether a delirium, yet it has many points
in common therewith. I call it rather a discerning of the infinite
in the finite—of the ideal made real. *Carlyle.*

It is better to have loved and lost,
Than never to have loved at all. *Tennyson.*

Love is life's end! an end, but never ending;
All joys, all sweets, all happiness, awarding;
Love is life's wealth, (ne'er spent, but ever spending,)
More rich by giving, taking by discarding;
Love's life's reward, rewarding in rewarding;
Then from thy wretched heart fond care remove;
Ah! shouldst thou live but once love's sweets to prove,
Thou wilt not love to live, unless thou live to live. *Spenser.*

Let none think to fly the danger
For soon or late love is his own avenger. *Byron.*

Love that has nothing but beauty to keep it in good health
is short lived, and apt to have ague fits. *Erasmus.*

But love is blind, and lovers cannot see
The pretty follies that themselves commit. *Shakespeare.*

Love's a capricious power; I've known it hold
  Out through a fever caused by its own heat;
But be much puzzled by a cough or cold,
  And find a quinsy very hard to treat. *Byron.*

Love not! love not! the thing you love may change,
  The rosy lip may cease to smile on you,
The kindly beaming eye grow cold and strange,
  The heart still warmly beat, and not for you.

Mrs. Norton.

The more we love the nearer we are to hate.

La Rochefoucauld.

I know a passion still more deeply charming
That fever'd youth e'er felt; and that is love,
By long experience mellow'd into friendship. *Thomson.*

151

She never told her love,
But let concealment, like a worm in the bud
Feed on her damask cheek; she pined in thought;
And, with a green and yellow melancholy
She sat like patience on a monument,
Smiling at grief. *Shakespeare.*

Love me little, love me long. *Marlowe.*

Love will find its way
Through paths where wolves would fear to prey,
And if it dares enough 'twere hard
If passion met not some reward. *Byron.*

For the memory of live is sweet,
   Though the love itself were vain
And what I have lost of pleasure,
   Assuage what I find of pain. *Lyster.*

Love is a god
Strong, free, unbounded, and as some define
Fears nothing, pitieth none. *Milton.*

O! love is like the rose,
   And a month it may not see,
Ere it withers where it grows. *Bailey.*

For oh! so wildly do I love him
That paradise itself were dim
And joyless, if not shared with him. *Moore.*

Love is not in our choice, but in our fate. *Dryden.*

Who loves, raves—'tis youth's phrenzy; but the cure
Is bitterer still. *Byron.*

Love is a passion
Which kindles honor into noble acts. *Dryden.*

Nuptial love maketh mankind, friendly love perfecteth it;
but wanton love corrupteth and embaseth it. *Bacon.*

It warms me, it charms me,
   To mention but her name;
It heats me, it beats me,
   And set me a' on flame. *Burns.*

All the passions make us commit faults; love makes us commit the most ridiculous ones. *La Rochefoucauld.*

Men have died from time to time, and worms have eaten them, but not for love. *Shakespeare.*

To write a good love-letter you ought to begin without knowing what you mean to say, and to finish without knowing what you have written. *Rousseau.*

Love's like the measles—all the worse when it comes late in life. *Jerrola.*

Love is merely madness; and I tell you, deserves as well a dark house and a whip, as madmen do; and the reason why they are not so punished and cured, is that the lunacy is so ordinary, that the whippers are in love too. *Shakespeare.*

If you cannot inspire a woman with love of you, fill her above the brim with love of herself;—all that runs over will be yours. *Colton.*

A mother's love!
If there be one thing pure,
Where all beside is sullied,
That can endure,
When all else passes away;
If there be aught
Surpassing human deed or word, or thought,
 It is a mother's love. *Marchioness de Spadara.*

What *is* mother's love?
A noble, pure, and tender flame
Enkindled from above. *James Montgomery.*

Love moderately; long love doth so;
Too swift arrives as tardy as too slow. *Shakespeare.*

When love's well-timed, 'tis not a fault to love;
The strong, the brave, the virtuous, and the wise,
Sink in the soft captivity together. *Addison.*

 Love did his reason blind,
And love's the noblest frailty of the mind. *Dryden.*

Love is a pearl of purest hue,

But stormy waves are round it;
And dearly may a woman rue,
   The hour that first she found it.   *L. E. Landon.*

When poverty comes in at the door, love flies out at the window.   *Anon.*

No cord or cable can draw so forcible, or bind so fast, as love can do with only a single thread.   *Burton.*

Man while he loves, is never quite depraved,
And woman's triumph is a lover saved.   *Lamb.*

Is there no way to bring home a wandering sheep, but by worrying him to death?   *Fuller.*

To love and to be wise is scarcely granted to the highest.
   Laberius.

Love, the sole disease thou canst not cure.   *Pope.*

Who ever loved that loved not at first sight?   *Marlowe.*

Love is strong as death. Many waters cannot quench love, neither can the floods drown it; if a man would give all the substance of his house for love, it would utterly be contemned.
   Solomon's Song viii, 6, 7.

To her love was like the air of heaven—invisible, intangible; it yet encircled her soul, and she knew it; for in it was her life.   *Miss M'Intosh.*

All thoughts, all passions, all delights,
Whatever stirs this mortal frame,
All are but ministers of love,
And feed his sacred flame.   *Coleridge.*

The first symptom of love in a young man is timidity, in a girl it is boldness. The two sexes have a tendency to approach, and each assumes the qualities of the other.   *Victor Hugo.*

That you may be loved be amiable.   *Ovid.*

All love at first, like gen'rous wine,
Ferments and frets until 'tis fine,
But when 'tis settled on the lee,
And from the impurer matter free,

Becomes the richer still the older.
And proves the pleasanter the colder.   *Butler.*

The proverb holds, that to be wise and love,
Is hardly granted to the gods above.   *Dryden.*

Alas! the love of women! it is known
To be a lovely and a fearful thing;
For all of theirs upon that die is thrown,
And if 'tis lost, life has no more to bring
To them but mockeries of the past alone.   *Byron.*

      The wound's invisible
That love's keen arrows make.   *Shakespeare.*

LOVE AND FRIENDSHIP.

Friendship often ends in love; but love in friendship never.
Colton.

LOVER.

If I freely may discover
What should please me in my lover,
I would have her fair and witty,
Savouring more of court than city;
A little proud, but full of pity;
Light and humorous in her toying,
Oft building hopes, and soon destroying,
Long, but sweet in the enjoying;
Neither too easy nor too hard;
All extremes I would have bar'd.   *Ben Jonson.*

A lover's like a hunter—if the game be got with too much
ease he cares not for't.   *Mead.*

In lover's quarrels, the party that loves most is always most
willing to acknowledge the greater fault.   *Scott.*

Doubt thou the stars are fire!
Doubt that the sun doth move;
Doubt truth to be a liar;
But never doubt I love.   *Shakespeare.*

155

A reserved lover, it is said, always makes a suspicious husband. *Goldsmith.*

> Yet, if thou swear'st,
> Thou may'st prove false; at lover's vows,
> They say, Jove laughs. *Shakespeare.*

O, men's vows are women's traitors. *Shakespeare.*

LUST.

> Capricious, wanton, bold, and brutal lust
> Is meanly selfish; when resisted, cruel;
> And, like the blast of pestilential winds,
> Taints the sweet bloom of nature's fairest forms. *Milton.*

LUXURY.

> War destroys men, but luxury mankind
> At once corrupts the body and the mind. *Crown.*

LYING.

> And he that does one fault at first,
> And lies to hide it, makes it two. *Isaac Watts.*

He who has not a good memory, should never take upon him the trade of lying. *Montaigne.*

MADNESS.

> How pregnant, sometimes, his replies are!
> A happiness that often madness hits on,
> Which sanity and reason could not be
> So prosp'rously deliver'd of. *Shakespeare.*

> I am not mad; I would to heaven I were!
> For then, 'tis like I should forget myself;
> O, if I could, what grief should I forget! *Shakespeare.*

> There is a pleasure in being mad,
> Which none but madmen know. *Dryden.*

Great wits are sure to madness near allied,
And thin partitions do their bounds divide.   *Dryden.*

MAIDEN.

Maidens, like moths, are ever caught by glare,
And mammon wins his way where seraphs might despair.
Byron.

A child no more! a maiden now—
A graceful maiden, with a gentle brow;
A cheek tinged lightly and a dove-like eye;
And all hearts bless her as she passes by.   *Mary Howitt.*

MAIN CHANCE.

As the ancients say wisely
Have a care o' th' main chance;
And look before you ere you leap;
For as you sow, y' are like to reap.   *Butler.*

MAN.

God made him, and therefore let him pass for a man.
Shakespeare.

Like a man made after supper of a cheese-paring; when
he was naked, he was, for all the world, like a forked radish,
with a head fantastically carved upon it with a knife.
Shakespeare.

Know thou this:——that men
Are as the time is.   *Shakespeare.*

What a piece of work is man! How noble in reason; how
infinite in faculties; in form and moving, how express and ad-
mirable! In action, how like an angel; in apprehension, how like
a god; the beauty of the world—the paragon of animals! And
yet to me what is this quintessence of dust?   *Shakespeare.*

Every man is a volume, if you know how to read him.
Channing.

Men are but children of a larger growth.   *Dryden.*

He is the whole encyclopedia of facts. The creation of a thousand forests is in one acorn; and Egypt, Greece, Rome, Gaul, Britain, America, lie folded already in the first man.

Emerson.

Men are machines, with all their boasted freedom,
Their movements turn upon some favorite passion;
Let art but find the foible out,
We touch the spring and wind them at our pleasure.

Brooke.

The way to conquer men is by their passions;
Catch but the ruling foibles of their hearts,
And all their boasted virtues shrink before you. *Tolson.*

A man he seems of cheerful yesterdays and confident to-morrows.

Wordsworth.

Men are born with *two* eyes, but with *one* tongue, in order that they should see twice as much as they say. *Colton.*

The mind of man is vastly like a hive;
His thoughts are busy ever—all alive;
  But here the simile will go no further;
For bees are making honey, one and all;
Man's thoughts are busy in producing gall,
  Committing, as it were, self-murther. *Dr. Wolcot.*

O man! while in the early years,
  How prodigal of time,
Misspending all thy precious hours,
  Thy glorious youthful prime!
Alternate follies take the sway;
  Licentious passions burn;
Which tenfold force give nature's law,
  That man was made to mourn. *Burns.*

Beware the fury of a patient man. *Dryden.*

Know then thyself; presume not God to scan;
The proper study of mankind is man. *Pope.*

MANNERS.

Of manners gentle, of affections mild;
In wit a man, simplicity a child. *Pope.*

Evil habits soil a fine dress more than mud; good manners, by their deeds, easily set off a lowly garb.   *Plautus.*

Nothing so much prevents our being natural as the desire of appearing so.   *La Rochefoucauld.*

Those that are good manners at the court are as ridiculous in the country, as the behavior of the country is most mockable at the court.   *Shakespeare.*

MARRIAGE.

Hail, wedded love, mysterious law, true source
Of human offspring, sole propriety
In paradise of all things common else!   *Milton.*

The best time for marriage will be towards thirty, for as the younger times are unfit, either to choose or to govern a wife and family, so, if thou stay long, thou shalt hardly see the education of thy children, who, being left to strangers, are in effect lost; and better were it to be unborn than ill-bred; for thereby thy posterity shall either perish or remain a shame to thy name.   *Sir Walter Raleigh.*

Domestic happiness, thou only bliss
Of paradise that has survived the fall.   *Cowper.*

Marriage is a feast where the grace is sometimes better than the feast.   *Colton.*

The moment a woman marries, some terrible revolution happens in her system; all her good qualities vanish, presto, like eggs out of a conjuror's box. 'Tis true that they appear on the other side of the box, but for the husband they are gone forever.   *Bulwer.*

First get an absolute conquest over thyself, and then thou wilt easily govern thy wife.   *Fuller.*

MASTERS AND SERVANTS.

If thou art a master, be sometimes blind; if a servant, sometimes deaf.   *Fuller.*

MAXIMS.

Maxims are the condensed good sense of nations.

Sir J. Mackintosh.

MEDICINES.

Joy, temperance, and repose,
Slam the door on the doctor's nose.   *Longfellow.*

MEDIOCRITY.

Persevering mediocrity is much more respectable, and unspeakably more useful than talented inconstancy.

Dr. James Hamilton.

MEDITATION.

Though reading and conversation may furnish us with many ideas of men and things, yet it is our own meditation must form our judgment.   *Dr. I. Watts.*

MELANCHOLY.

Melancholy is the nurse of frenzy.   *Shakespeare.*

Go, you may call it madness, folly,—
    You shall not chase my gloom away;
There's such a charm in melancholy,
    I would not, if I could, be gay!   *Rogers.*

Melancholy
Sits on me, as a cloud along the sky,
Which will not let the sunbeams through, nor yet
Descend in rain, and end, but spreads itself
Twixt heaven and earth, like envy between man
And man—an everlasting mist.   *Byron.*

MEMORY.

Lull'd in the countless chambers of the brain,
Our thoughts are link'd by many a hidden chain;

Awake but one, and lo, what myriads rise!
Each stamps its image as the other flies.   *Pope.*

Tears, idle tears, I know not what they mean,
Tears from the depth of some divine despair,
Rise in the heart and gather in the eyes,
In looking on the happy autmn fields
And thinking of the days that are no more. *Tennyson.*

A strong memory is generally coupled with an infirm judgment.   *Montaigne.*

MEN.

Men are the sport of circumstances, when the circumstances
seem the sport of men.   *Byron.*

There are but three classes of men: *the retrograde, the
stationary* and *the progressive.*   *Lavater.*

It is far easier to know men than to know man.
                                        La Rochefoucauld.

Never have anything to do with an unlucky place, or an
unlucky man. I have seen many clever men, very clever men,
who had not shoes to their feet. I never act with them. Their
advice sounds very well, but they cannot get on themselves; and
if they cannot do good to themselves, how can they do good to
me?   *Rothschild.*

MEN, GREAT.

Lives of great men all remind us,
    We can make our lives sublime,
And departing, leave behind us
    Footprints in the sands of time.

Footprints, that perhaps another,
    Sailing o'er life's solemn main,
A forlorn and shipwreck'd brother,
    Seeing, shall take heart again.   *Longfellow.*

161

MERCY.

The quality of mercy is not strain'd:
It droppeth, as the gentle rain from heaven
Upon the place beneath; it is twice bless'd,
It blesseth him that gives, and him that takes:
'Tis mightiest in the mightiest: it becomes
The throned monarch better than his crown:
His sceptre shows the force of temporal power,
The attribute to awe and majesty,
Wherein doth sit the dread and fear of kings;
But mercy is above this scepter'd sway,
It is an attribute to God himself;
And earthly power doth then show likest God's,
When mercy seasons justice.
 *   *   *   consider this,—
That, in the course of justice, none of us
Should see salvation: we do pray for mercy;
And that same prayer doth teach us all to render
The deeds of mercy.   *Shakespeare.*

MERIT.

Modesty is to merit as shades to figures in a picture; giving
it strength and beauty.   *La Bruyère.*

Good actions crown themselves with lasting bays
Who deserves well, needs not another's praise.   *Heath.*

METAPHYSICS.

He knew what's what, and that's as high
As metaphysics' wit can fly.   *Meta.*

MIDNIGHT.

Midnight,—strange mystic hour,—when the veil between the
frail present and the eternal future grows thin.   *Mrs. Stowe.*

MIND.

My mind to me an empire is   *Southwell.*

162

In my mind's eye, Horatio.   *Shakespeare.*

A mind content both crown and kingdom is.   *Greene.*

Cultivation to the mind is as necessary as food to the body.
                                             Cicero.

Canst thou not minister to a mind diseased;
Pluck from the memory a rooted sorrow;
Raze out the written troubles of the brain;
And, with some sweet oblivious antidote,
Cleanse the foul bosom of that perilous stuff
Which weighs upon the heart?   *Shakespeare.*

'Tis the mind that makes the body rich.   *Shakespeare.*

It is the mind that maketh good or ill,
That maketh wretch or happy, rich or poor.   *Spenser.*

A narrow mind begets obstinacy, and we do not easily believe what we cannot see.   *Dryden.*

The mind ought sometimes to be diverted, that it may return the better to thinking.   *Phoedrus.*

A weak mind is like a microscope, which magnifies trifling things, but cannot receive great ones.   *Chesterfield.*

            Ah! noblest minds
Sink soonest into ruin; like a tree,
That with the weight of its own golden fruitage
Is bent down to the dust.   *H. Neele.*

MINISTER.

Of right and wrong he taught
Truths as refined as ever Athens heard;
And (strange to tell!) he practised what he preach'd
                                             Armstrong.

The life of a pious minister is visible rhetoric.   *Hooker.*

It would be well, if some who have taken upon themselves the ministry of the Gospel, that they would first preach to themselves, then afterwards to others.   *Cardinal Pole.*

MIRTH.

O spirits gay, and kindly heart!
Precious the blessings ye impart!   *Joanna Baillie.*

From the crown of his head to the sole of his foot he is
all mirth; he has twice or thrice cut Cupid's bowstring, and the
little hangman dare not shoot at him: he hath a heart as sound
as a bell, and his tongue is the clapper; for what his heart
thinks his tongue speaks.   *Shakespeare.*

Jest and youthful jollity,
Quips, and cranks, and wanton wiles,
Nods and becks, and wreathed smiles.   *Milton.*

Care to our coffin adds a nail, no doubt;
And ev'ry grin so merry, draws on out.   *Dr. Wolcot.*

MISANTHROPE.

I am *misanthropos,* and hate mankind.
For thy part, I do wish thou wert a dog,
That I might love thee something.   *Shakespeare.*

As prone to mischief, as able to perform it.   *Shakespeare*

MISER.

Some o'er-enamour'd of their bags, run mad;
Groan under gold, yet weep for want of bread.   *Young.*

I can compare our rich misers to nothing so fitly as to a
whale; that plays and tumbles, driving the poor fry before him,
and at last devours them all at a mouthful.   *Shakespeare.*

MISERY.

This iron world
Brings down the stoutest hearts to lowest state:
For misery doth bravest minds abate.   *Spenser.*

MISFORTUNE.

Misfortune, like a creditor severe,
But rises in demand for her delay;

She makes a scourge of past prosperity
To sting thee more and double thy distress.   *Young.*

MISTRUST.

I hold it cowardice,
To rest mistrustful, where a noble heart
Hath pawn'd an open hand in sign of love.   *Shakespeare.*

It is more disgraceful to distrust than to be deceived by
our friends.   *La Rochefoucauld.*

The world is an old woman, that mistakes any gilt farthing
for a gold coin; whereby being often cheated, she will hence-
forth trust nothing but the common copper.   *Carlyle.*

MODESTY.

The crimson glow of modesty o'erspread
Her cheek, and gave new lustre to her charms.
                          Dr. Thomas Franklin.

The violet droops its soft and bashful brow,
    But from its heart sweet incense fills the air;—
So rich within—so pure without—art thou,
    With modest mien and soul of virtue rare.   *Mrs. Osgood.*

They oft-times take more pains
Who look for pins, than those who find out stars.
                          John Fountain.

MOMENTS.

Think nought a trifle,though it small appear;
Small sands the mountain, moments make the year,
And trifles life.   *Young.*

MONEY.

If you make money your god, it will plague you like the
devil.   *Fielding.*

Mammon has enriched his thousands, and has damned his ten thousands. *South.*

The love of money is the root of all evil; which while some coveted after they have erred from the faith, and pierced themselves through with many sorrows. I *Tim.* vi, 10.

For they say, if money go before, all ways do lie open. *Shakespeare.*

Money is a good servant, but a dangerous master. *Bonhours.*

Put not your trust in money, but put your money in trust. *Holmes.*

He that wants money, means and content, is without three good friends. *Shakespeare.*

MOON.

The cold chaste Moon, the Queen of Heaven's bright isles,
Who makes all beautiful on which she smiles!
That wandering shrine of soft, yet icy flame,
Which ever is trasnform'd yet still the same,
And warms, but not illumines. *Shelley.*

The queen of night
Shines fair with all her virgin stars about her. *Otway.*

Now through the passing clouds she seems to stoop,
Now up the pure cerulean rides sublime.
Wide the pale deluge floats, and streaming mild
O'er the sky'd mountain to the shadowy vale,
While rocks and floods reflect the quivering gleam,
The whole air whitens with a boundless tide
Of silver radiance, trembling round the world. *Thomson.*

MORAL LAW.

The moral law is written on the tablets of eternity. For every false word or unrighteous deed, for cruelty and oppression, for lust or vanity, the price has to be paid at last. *J. A. Froude.*

166

MORNING

But, look, the morn in russet mantle clad
Walks o'er the dew of yon high eastern hill   *Shakespeare.*

Now from night's womb the glorious day breaks forth,
And seems to kindle from the setting stars.   *Lee.*

Morn, in the white wake of the morning star,
Came furrowing all the orient into gold.   *Tennyson.*

Now morn her rosy steps in th' eastern clime
Advancing, sow'd the earth with orient pearl.   *Milton.*

MOTHER.

She was my friend—I had but her—no more,
No other upon earth—and as for heaven,
I am as they that seek a sign, to whom
No sign is given. My mother! Oh, my mother!   *Taylor.*

A mother is a mother still,
The holiest thing alive.   *Coleridge.*

MOURNING.

None acted mourning forced to show,
Or squeeze his eyes to make the torrent flow.   *Dryden.*

Excess of grief for the deceased is madness; for it is an
injury to the living, and the dead know it not. *Xenophon.*

MURMURING.

Murmur at nothing: if our ills are reparable, it is un-
grateful; if remediless, it is vain.   *Shakespeare.*

MUSIC.

The man that hath no music in himself,
Nor is not moved with concord of sweet sounds,
Is fit for treasons, stratagems and spoils;
The motions of his spirit are dull as night,
And his affections dark as Erebus;

Let no such man be trusted.   *Shakespeare.*

Music hath charms to soothe a savage breast,
To soften rocks, or bend a knotted oak.
I've read that things inanimate have moved,
And as with living souls have been inform'd
By magic numbers and persuasive sound.   *Congreve.*

There's music in the sighing of a reed;
There's music in the gushing of a rill;
There's music in all things, if men had ears
Their earth is but an echo of the spheres.   *Byron.*

NAME.

He left a name, at which the world grew pale,
To point a moral, or adorn a tale.   *Johnson.*

NATURE.

The sea is like a silvery lake,
    And o'er its calm the vessel glides
Gently as if it fear'd to wake
    The slumbers of the silent tides.   *Moore.*

Man's rich with little, were his judgment true;
Nature is frugal, and her wants are few;
These few wants, answer'd bring sincere delights;
But fools create themselves new appetites.   *Young.*

All things are artificial, for
Nature is the art of God.   *Sir Thos. Browne.*

Surely there is something in the unruffled calm of nature
that owerawes our little anxieties and doubts: the sight of the
deep-blue sky, and the clustering stars above, seems to impart
a quiet to the mind.   *Edwards.*

To him who in the love of nature holds
Communion with her visible forms, she speaks
A various language.   *Bryant.*

Nature the vicar of the Almighty Lord.   *Chaucer.*

168

One impulse from a vernal wood
  May teach you more of man,
Of moral evil and of good,
  Than all the sages can.   *Wordsworth.*

NATURE AND ART.

Nature is mighty. Art is mighty. Artifice is weak. For nature is the work of a mightier power than man. Art is the work of man under the guidance and inspiration of a mightier power. Artifice is the work of mere man in the imbecility of his mimic understanding.   *Anon.*

Nature is the chart of God, mapping out all His attributes; art is the shadow of His wisdom, and copieth His resources.

Tupper.

NECESSITY.

The tyrant's plea.   *Milton.*

When fear admits no hope of safety,
Necessity makes dastards valiant men.   *Herricks.*

Necessity is the mother of invention.

NECK.

A lover forsaken
  A new love may get;
But a neck that's once broken
  Can never be set.   *Walsh.*

NEGLIGENCE.

A little fire is quickly trodden out;
Which being suffer'd, rivers cannot quench. *Shakespeare.*

Omittance is no quittance.   *Shakespeare.*

NEGOTIATION

It is better to sound a person with whom one deals afar off, than to fall upon the point at first.   *Bacon.*

NERVOUSNESS.

He experienced that nervous agitation to which brave men as well as cowards are subject; with this difference, that the one sinks under it, like the vine under the hailstorm, and the other collects his energies to shake it off, as the cedar of Lebanon is said to elevate its boughs to disperse the snow which accumulate upon them. *Sir Walter Scott.*

NEWS.

Nothing is new; we walk where others went;
There's no vice now but has its precedent. *Herrick.*

NEWS.

For evil news rides post, while good news baits. *Milton.*

NEWSPAPERS.

An abstract and brief chronicle of the times.
Every editor of newspapers pays tribute to the Devil.
La Fontaine.

NICKNAME.

A nickname is the heaviest stone the devil can throw at a man. *Anon.*

A good name will wear out; a bad one may be turned; a nickname lasts forever. *Zimmerman.*

NIGHT.

Night whose sable hand
Hangs on the purple skirts of flying day. *Dyer.*

Why does the evening, does the night, put warmer love in our hearts? Is it the nightly pressure of helplessness? or is it the exalting separation from the turmoils of life, that veiling of the world in which for the soul nothing there remains but souls? Is it therefore that the letters in which the loved name stands written in our spirit appears like phosphorous writing by night, *in fire,* were by day, in their cloudy traces, they but smoke?

Richter.

How like a widow in her weeds, the night,
Amid her glimmering tapers, silent sits!
How sorrowful, how desolate, she weeps
Perpetual dews, and saddens nature's scene.   *Young.*

       In her starry shade
Of dim and solitary loveliness,
I learn the language of another world.   *Byron.*

NOBILITY.

Better not be at all,
Than not be noble.   *Tennyson.*

Would'st thou clearly learn what true nobility is? inquire of noble-minded women.   *German saying.*

He is noble only who in word, thought and deed, proves himself a man.   *Anon.*

NONSENSE.

A little nonsense now and then,
Is relish'd by the best of men.   *Anon.*

Nonsense and noise will oft prevail,
When honor and affection fail.   *Lloyd.*

NOVELS.

Writers of novels and romances in general bring a double loss on their readers, they rob them both of their time and money; representing men, manners, and things, that never have been, nor are likely to be; either confounding or perverting history or truth, inflating the mind, or committing violence upon the understanding.   *Lady Montague.*

NOVELTY.

Of all the passions that possess mankind,
The love of novelty rules most the mind;

171

In search of this, from realm to realm we roam;
Our fleets come fraught with ev'ry folly home.   *Foote.*

NOW.

Now! it is gone.—Our brief hours travel post,
Each with its thought or deed, its why or how;
But know, each parting hour gives up a ghost
To dwell within thee—an eternal now!   *Coleridge.*

OAK.

The monarch oak, the patriarch of the trees,
Shoots rising up, and spreads by slow degrees:
Three centuries he grows, and three he stays
Supreme in state; and in three more decays.   *Dryden.*

OATHS.

An oath is a recognizance to heaven,
Binding us over in the courts above,
To plead to the indictment of our crimes,
That those who 'scape this world should suffer there.
Southern.

I'll take thy word for faith, not ask thine oath;
Who shuns not to break one, will sure crack both.
Shakespeare.

OBEDIENCE.

I hourly learn a doctrine of obedience.   *Shakespeare.*

Wicked men obey for fear, but the good for love.
Aristotle.

Let them obey that know not how to rule.   *Shakespeare.*

OBLIGATION.

An extraordinary haste to discharge an obligation is a sort
of ingratitude.   *La Rochefoucauld.*

172

OBSERVATION.

He alone is an acute observer who can observe minutely without being observed.   *Lavater.*

OBSTINACY.

Narrowness of mind is often the cause of obstinacy: we do not easily believe beyond what we see.   *La Rochefoucauld.*

An obstinate man does not hold opinions, but they hold him.   *Pope.*

Stiff opinion, always in the wrong.   *Dryden.*

OCCASION.

Let me not let pass
Occasion, which now smiles.   *Milton.*

OCEAN.

Whosoever commands the sea commands the trade; whosoever commands the trade of the world commands the riches of the world, and, consequently, the world itself.
                    Sir Walter Raleigh.

OFFENCE.

Who fears t' offend takes the first step to please.   *Cibber.*

Offences ought to be pardoned, for few offend willingly, but as they are compelled by some affection.   *Hegesippus.*

At every trifle scorn to take offence,
That always shews great pride or little sense.   *Pope.*

OMISSIONS.

Omissions, no less than commissions, are often times branches of injustice.   *Antoninus.*

OPINIATORS.

There are a sort of men, whose visages
Do cream and mantle, like a standing pond;
And do a wilful stillness entertain,
With purpose to be dress'd in an opinion
Of wisdom, gravity, profound conceit;
As who should say, *I am Sir Oracle,*
And, when I ope my lips, let no dog bark?
    . . .   I do know of these
That therefore only are reputed wise.
For saying nothing.   *Shakespeare.*

OPINION.

Opinion, the blind goddess of fools, foe
To the virtuous, and only friend to
Undeserving persons.   *Chapman.*

If a man would register all his opinions upon love, politics, religion, and learning, what a bundle of inconsistencies and contradictions would appear at last!   *Swift.*

Opinion, that great fool, makes fools of all.   *Field.*

There's nothing good or bad, but thinking makes it so.
                               Shakespeare.

Opinion is that high and mighty dame
Which rules the world; and in the mind doth frame
Distaste or liking: for in human race,
She makes the fancy various as the face.   *Howel.*

OPINIONS.

He that never changed any of his opinions never corrected any of his mistakes; and he who was never wise enough to find out any mistakes in himself will not be charitable enough to excuse what he reckons mistakes in others.

OPPORTUNITY.

There is a tide in the affairs of men,
Which, taken at the flood, leads on to fortune;

Omitted, all the voyage of their life
Is bound in shallows and in miseries:
On such a full sea are we now afloat,
And we must take the current when it serves,
Or lose our ventures.   *Shakespeare.*

Opportunity has hair in front, behind she is bald; if you seize her by the forelock, you may hold her, but, if suffered to escape, not Jupiter himself can catch her again.
                                             From the Latin.

There sometimes wants only a stroke of fortune to discover numberless latent good or bad qualities, which would otherwise have been eternally concealed: as words written with a certain liquor appear only when applied to the fire.   *Greville.*

OPPOSED.

Equally to God and truth opposed;
Opposed as darkness to the light of heaven.   *Pollok.*

ORATOR.

What the orators want in depth, they give you in length.
                                             Montesquieu.

Fire in each eye, and papers in each hand,
They rave, recite, and madden round the land.   *Pope.*

ORDER.

Order is the sanity of the mind, the health of the body, the peace of the city, the security of the state. As the beams to a house, as the bones to the microcosm of man, so is order to all things.
                                             Southey.

Order is heaven's first law; and this confest,
Some are, and must be, greater than the rest,
More rich, more wise; but who infers from hence
That such are happier, shocks all common sense.   *Pope.*

ORIGINALITY.

The little mind who loves itself, will write and think with the vulgar; but the great mind will be bravely eccentric, and scorn the beaten road, from universal benevolence. *Goldsmith.*

ORPHAN.

An orphan's curse would drag to hell
A spirit from on high. *Coleridge.*

PAIN.

Long pains, with use of bearing, are half eased. *Dryden.*

PARASITE.

Your friend, your pimp, your hanger-on, what not?
Your lacquey, but without the shoulder-knot. *Horace.*

PARDON.

Pardon, I beseech Thee, the iniquity of this people, according unto the greatness of Thy mercy! And the Lord said I have pardoned, according to thy word. *Numbers* xiv, 19.

Thou art a God ready to pardon, gracious and merciful, slow to anger, and of great kindness. *Nehemiah* ix, 17.

PARENTS.

A suspicious parent makes an artful child. *Haliburton.*

PARTING.

Abruptness is an eloquence in parting, when spinning out the time is but the weaving of new sorrow. *Sir John Suckling.*

'to die and part
Is a less evil; but to part and live,
There—there's the torment. *Lansdowne.*

Farewell; God knows, when we shall meet again,
I have a faint cold, fear thrills through my veins,
That almost freezes up the heat of life.   *Shakespeare.*

My heart is heavy at the remembrance of all the miles that
lie between us; and I can scarcely believe that you are so distant
from me. We are parted; and every parting is a form of death,
as every re-union is a type of heaven.   *Edwards.*

Good night, good night! parting is such sweet sorrow
That I shall say good night till it be morrow.   *Shakespeare.*

PASSION.

How terrible is passion! how our reason
Falls down before it! whilst the tortur'd frame,
Like a ship dash'd by fierce encount'ring tides,
And of her pilot spoil'd, drives round and round,
The sport of wind and wave.   *Barford.*

The ruling passion, be it what it will,
The ruling passion conquers reason still.   *Pope.*

PASSIONS.

Passion often makes a madman of the cleverest man, and
renders the greatest fools clever.
  The passions are the only orators that always persuade.
  The passions often engender their contraries.
                              La Rochefoucauld.

Passions, like seas, will have their ebbs and flows.   *Lee.*

The wither'd frame, the ruin'd mind,
The wreck by passion left behind;
A shrivell'd scroll, a scatter'd leaf,
Sear'd by the autumn-blast of grief.   *Byron.*

Our passions are like convulsion fits, which, though they
make us stronger for a time, leave us the weaker ever after.
                              Pope.

The passions, like heavy bodies down steep hills, once in

motion, move themselves, and know no ground but the bottom.

Fuller.

Oh! she has passions which outstrip the wind,
And tear her virtue up, as tempests root the sea.

Congreve.

PATIENCE.

If the wicked flourish, and thou suffer, be not discouraged.
They are fatted for destruction: thou art dieted for health.

Fuller.

Patience is sorrow's salve.   *Churchill.*

There is a limit at which forbearance ceases to be a virtue.

Burke.

He that would have a cake out of the wheat must tarry
the grinding.   *Shakespeare.*

PATRIOT.

Who, firmly good in a corrputed state,
Against the rage of tyrants singly stood,
Invincible.   *Thomson.*

'Tis home-felt pleasure prompts the patriot's sigh
This makes him wish to live, and dare to die.   *Campbell.*

PEACE.

Down the dark future, through long generations,
The echoing sounds grow fainter and then cease;
And like a bell, with solemn, sweet vibrations,
I hear once more the voice of Christ say "Peace!"

Longfellow.

Peace hath her victories,
No less renown'd than war.   *Milton.*

PEACEMAKERS.

Blessed are the peacemakers, for they shall be called the
children of God.   *St. Matthew* v, 9.

PEDANTRY.

Brimful of learning, see that pedant stride,
Bristling with horrid Greek, and puff'd with pride!
A thousand authors he in vain has read,
And with their maxims stuff'd his empty head;
And thinks that without Aristotle's rule,
Reason is blind, and common sense a fool!   *Boileau.*

Pedantry crams our heads with learned lumber, and takes
out our brains to make room for it.   *Colton.*

PEN.

Oh! nature's noblest gift—my grey goose quill:
Slave of my thoughts, obedient to my will,
Torn from thy parent bird to form a pen,
That mighty instrument of little men!   *Byron.*

PENETRATION.

The balls of sight are so formed, that one man's eyes are
spectacles to another, to read his heart within.   *Johnson.*

PENURY.

Chill penury weighs down the heart, itself; and though it
sometimes be endured with calmness, it is but the calmness of
despair.   *Mrs. Jameson.*

PEOPLE.

The world may be divided into people that read, people
that write, people that think, and fox hunters.   *Shenstone.*

PERFECTION.

To arrive at perfection, a man should have very sincere
friends or inveterate enemies; because he would be made sensible of his good or ill conduct, either by the censures of the
one, or the admonitions of the other.   *Diogenes.*

PERSEVERANCE.

Yet I argue not
Against heaven's hand or will, nor bate a jot
Of heart or hope, but still bear up and steer
Right onward.   *Milton.*

When I take the humor of a thing once, I am like your
tailor's needle—I go through.   *Ben Jonson.*

By gnawing through a dyke even a rat may drown a nation.
Edward Burke.

Let us only suffer any person to tell us his story morning
and evening, but for one twelve-month, and he will become our
master.   *Burke.*

PERSEVERANCE AND OBSTINACY.

The difference between perseverance and obstinancy is that
one often comes from a strong will, and the other from a strong
won't.

PERVERSITY.

Some men put me in mind of half-bred horses, which often
grow worse in proportion as you feed and exercise them for
improvement.   *Greville.*

PHILOSOPHY.

Philosophy, when superficially studied, excites doubt; when
thoroughly explored, it dispels it.   *Bacon.*

A little philosophy inclineth man's mind to atheism, but
depth of philosophy bringeth a man's mind about to religion.
Bacon.

Do not all charms fly,
At the mere touch of cold philosophy?   *Keats.*

PHYSICIANS.

If you need a physician, employ these three—a cheerful
mind, rest, and a temperate diet.

The patient can oftener do without the doctor, than the doctor without the patient.   *Zimmerman.*

PHYSIOGNOMY.

As the language of the face is universal, so 'tis very comprehensive; no laconism can reach it: 'tis the short hand of the mind, and crowds a great deal in a little room.   *Jeremy Collier.*

PICTURE.

A picture is a poem without words.   *Horace.*

PITY.

The truly brave are soft of heart and eyes,
And feel for what their duty bids them do.   *Byron.*

No radiant pearl which crested fortune wears,
No gem that, twinkling, hangs from beauty's ears,
Not the bright stars which night's blue arch adorn,
Nor rising suns that gild the vernal morn,
Shine with such lustre as the tear that breaks
For other's woe, down virtue's manly cheeks.   *Darwin.*

Villian, thou know'st no law of God or man;
No beast so fierce, but knows some touch of pity.
                                                  Shakespeare.

PLAGIARISM.

It is one thing to purloin finely-tempered steel, and another to take a pound of literary old iron, and convert it in the furnace of one's mind into a hundred watchsprings, worth each a thousand times as much as the iron. When genius borrows, it borrows grandly, giving to the borrowed matter, a life and beauty it lacked before.   *Anon.*

PLEASURE.

The seeds of repentance are sown in youth by pleasure, but the harvest is reaped in age by pain.   *Colton.*

Enjoy your present pleasures so as not to injure those that are to follow. *Seneca.*

Flowers are like the pleasures of the world. *Shakespeare.*

Pleasure soon exhausts us and itself also; but endeavor never does. *Richter.*

Pleasure, or wrong or rightly understood,
Our greatest evil, or our greatest good. *Pope.*

Pleasure that comes unlooked for is thrice welcome.

Rogers.

Why, all delights are vain; but that most vain,
Which, with pain purchas'd, doth inherit pain.

Shakespeare.

PLEASURES.

Choose such pleasures as recreate much and cost little.
Fuller.

Put only the restriction on your pleasures—be cautious that they hurt no creature that has life. *Zimmerman.*

Venture not to the utmost bounds of even lawful pleasure; the limits of good and evil join. *Fuller.*

It is sad
To think how few our pleasures really are:
And for the which we risk eternal good. *Bailey.*

POET.

Just writes to make his barrenness appear,
And strain from hard-bound brains, eight lines a year.

Pope.

Poet! esteem thy noble part,
  Still listen, still record,
Sacred historian of the heart,
  And moral nature's lord. *Richard M. Milnes.*

POETRY.

Poetry is the eloquence of truth. *Campbell.*

Poetry has been to me "its own exceeding great reward;" it has soothed my afflictions; it has multiplied and refined my enjoyments; it has endeared solitude; and it has given me the habit of wishing to discover the good and the beautiful in all that meets and surrounds me. *Coleridge.*

POETS.

Poets are all who love—who feel great truths—
And tell them.

POLITENESS.

As charity covers a multitude of sins before God, so does politeness before men. *Chesterfield.*

When two goats met on a bridge which was too narrow to allow either to pass or return, the goat which lay down that the other might walk over it, was a finer gentleman than Lord Chesterfield. *Cecil.*

POLITIC.

The devil knew not what he did, when he made man politic. *Shakespeare.*

POLITICIAN.

A politician, Proteus-like must alter
His face, and habit; and, like water, seem
Of the same color that the vessel is
That doth contain it; varying his form
With the chameleon at each object's change. *Mason.*

POLITICS.

Who's in or out, who moves the grand machine,
Nor stirs my curiosity, or spleen;
Secrets of state no more I wish to know

183

Than secret movements of a puppet-show;
Let but the puppets move, I've my desire,
Unseen the hand which guides the master wire.

Churchill.

POPULARITY.

He who can listen pleas'd to such applause,
Buys at a dearer rate than I dare purchase,
And pays for idle air with sense and virtue.   *Mallett.*

Oh, popular applause, what heart of man
Is proof against thy sweet seducing charms?
The wisest and the best feel urgent need
Of all their caution in thy gentlest gales;
But swelled into a dust—who then, alas!
With all his canvas set, and inexpert
And therefore heedless can withstand thy power?

Cowper.

Please not thyself the flattering crowd to hear;
'Tis fulsome stuff to please thy itching ear.
Survey thy soul, not what thou dost appear,
But what thou art.   *Persius.*

POSSIBILITIES.

To him nothing is impossible, who is always dreaming of his past possibilities.   *Carlyle.*

POVERTY.

It is not poverty so much as pretence that harasses a ruined man—the struggle between a proud mind and an empty purse—the keeping up a hollow show that must soon come to an end. Have the courage to appear poor, and you disarm poverty to its sharpest sting.   *Mrs. Jameson.*

O blissful poverty!
Nature, too partial to thy lot, assigns
Health, freedom, innocence, and downy peace,

Her real goods; and only mocks the great
With empty pageantries.   *Fenton.*

This mournful truth is everywhere confessed.
Slow rises worth by poverty depressed.   *Johnson.*

He is poor whose expenses exceed his income.
                                               La Bruyère.

To mortal men great loads allotted be;
But of all packs no pack like poverty.   *Herrick.*

Poverty makes people satirical,—soberly, sadly, bitterly satirical.   *Friswell.*

POWER.

Nothing, indeed, but the possession of some power can with
any certainty discover what at the bottom is the true character
of any man.   *Burke.*

Even in war, moral power is to physical as three parts out
of four.   *Napoleon I.*

PRAISE.

Let another man praise thee, and not thine own mouth; a
stranger, and not thine own lips.   *Proverbs* xxvii, 2.

Allow no man to be so free with you as to praise you to
your face. Your vanity by this means will want its food. At the
same time your passion for esteem will be more fully grati-
fied; men will praise you in their actions: where you now receive one compliment, you will then receive twenty civilities.
                                               Steele.

Praise was originally a pension, paid by the world. *Swift.*

Those men who are commended by everybody, must be
very extraordinary men; or, which is more probable, very in-
considerable men.   *Greville.*

It gives me pleasure to be praised by you whom all men
praise.   *Tully.*

The more you speak of yourself, the more you are likely to lie.   *Zimmerman.*

There's not one wise man among twenty will praise himself.   *Shakespeare.*

PRAYER.

If any of you lack wisdom, let him ask of God, that giveth to all men liberally and upbraideth not; and it shall be given him. But let him ask in faith, nothing wavering. *James* i, 5, 6.

God is a spirit; and they that worship Him, must worship Him in spirit and in truth.   *St. John* iv, 24.

Ye ask, and receive not, because ye ask amiss.
James iv, 3.

He that cometh to God, must believe that He is, and that He is a rewarder of them that diligently seek Him.   *Heb.* xi, 6.

Fountain of mercy! whose pervading eye
Can look within and read what passes there,
Accept my thoughts for thanks; I have no words.
My soul o'erfraught with gratitude, rejects
The aid of language—Lord!—behold my heart.
Hannah More.

Prayer purifies; it is a self-preached sermon.   *Richter.*

Any heart turned Godward, feels more joy
In one short hour of prayer, than e'er was rais'd
By all the feasts on earth since their foundation.   *Bailey.*

More things are wrought by prayer
Than this world dreams of.   *Tennyson.*

In prayer it is better to have a heart without words, than words without a heart.   *Bunyan.*

Is not prayer a study of truth—a sally of the soul into the unfound infinite? No man ever prayed heartily without learning something; but when a faithful thinker resolute to detach every object from personal relations, and see it in the light of thought, shall, at the same time, kindle science with the fire of

186

the holiest affections, then with God go forth anew into the creation.   *Emerson.*

Let prayer be the key of the morning and the bolt of the evening.   *Matthew Henry.*

PREJUDICE.

To divest one's self of some prejudices, would be like taking off the skin to feel the better.   *Greville.*

PRESS.

"The Press!" all lands shall sing;
The press, the press we bring
   All lands to bless.
O pallid Want! O Labor stark!
Behold, we bring the second ark!
  The press! the press! the press!   *Ebenezer Elliot.*

PRESUMPTION.

Fools rush in where angels fear to tread.   *Pope.*

PRETENSION.

Where there is much pretension, much has been borrowed; nature never pretends.   *Lavater.*

It is no disgrace not to be able to do everything; but to undertake, or pretend to do, what you are not made for, is not only shameful, but extremely troublesome and vexatious.

Plutarch.

PRIDE.

The lofty pine is oftenest agitated by the wind—high towers rush to the earth with a heavier fall—and the lightning most frequently strikes the highest mountains.   *Horace.*

What is pride? a whizzing rocket
That would emulate a star.   *Wordsworth.*

Pride that dines on vanity sups on contempt. *B. Franklin.*

He whose pride oppresses the humble may, perhaps, be humbled, but will never be humble. *Lavater.*

Defeated, but not dismayed—crushed to the earth, but not humiliated,—he seemed to grow more haughty beneath disaster, and to experience a fierce satisfaction in draining the last dregs of bitterness. *Washington Irving.*

When pride begins, love ceases. *Lavater.*

The vile are only vain; the great are proud. *Byron.*

PRINCIPLES.

Let us cling to our principles as the mariner clings to his last plank when night and tempest close around him. *Anon.*

And oftener changed their principles than their shirts. *Dr. Young.*

PRISON.

A felon's cell—
The fittest earthy type of hell! *Whittier.*

Emblem of hell, nursery of vice. *Tom Brown.*

PROCRASTINATION.

Procrastination is the thief of time. *Dr. Young.*

Defer not till to-morrow to be wise,
To-morrow's sun to thee may never rise. *Congreve.*

PROGRESS.

Living movement. *Carlyle.*

The goal of yesterday will be the starting point of to-morrow. *Carlyle.*

PROMISES.

He who is most slow in making a promise, is the most faithful in the performance of it. *Rousseau.*

PROSPERITY.

Take care to be an economist in prosperity; there is no fear of your not being one in adversity.　　*Zimmerman.*

Knaves will thrive,
When honest plainness knows not how to live.　　*Shirley.*

Whilst you are prosperous you can number many friends; but when the storm comes you are left alone.　　*Ovid.*

PROVERBS.

The wisdom of many, and the wit of one.

Lord John Russell.

Jewels five-words long,
That on the stretch'd forefinger of all time
Sparkle forever.　　*Tennyson.*

PROVIDENCE.

The ways of heaven are dark and intricate,
Puzzled in mazes, and perplex'd with errors;
Our understanding traces them in vain,
Lost and bewilder'd in the fruitless search;
Nor sees with how much art the windings run,
Nor where the regular confusion ends.　　*Addison.*

How just is Providence in all its works.
How swift to overtake us in our crimes!　　*Lansdowne.*

PRUDENCE.

Men are born with two eyes, but with one tongue, in order that they should see twice as much as they say.　　*Colton.*

Want of prudence is too frequently the want of virtue; nor is there on earth a more powerful advocate for vice than poverty?　　*Goldsmith.*

PUNISHMENT.

Let rules be fix'd that may our rage contain,
And punish faults with a proportion'd pain;
And do not flay him, who deserves alone
A whipping for the fault that he has done.   *Horace.*

The seeds of our punishment are sown at the same time we commit sin.   *Hesiod.*

PURITY.

An angel might have stoop'd to see,
And bless'd her for her purity.   *Dr. Mackay.*

Purity is the feminine, truth the masculine, of honor.
     Hare.

PURSE.

                    Their love
Lies in their purses; and whoso empties them,
By so much fills their hearts with deadly hate.
     Shakespeare.

QUARRELS.

Those who in quarrels interpose,
Must often wipe a bloody nose.   *Gay.*

If he had two ideas in his head, they would fall out with each other.   *Johnson.*

I consider your very testy and quarrelsome people in the same light as I do a loaded gun, which may, by accident, go off and kill one.   *Shenstone.*

QUOTATIONS.

Some for renown on scraps of learning dote
And think they grow immortal as they quote.
To patchwork learn'd quotations are allied,
But strive to make our poverty our pride.   *Young.*

190

I am but a gatherer, and a disposer of other men's stuff.

Watton.

If the world like it not, so much the worse for them.

Cowper.

RABBLE.

They condemn what they do not understand.   *Cicero.*

A hundred mouths, a hundred tongues,
And throats of brass, inspired with iron lungs.   *Virgil.*

RAGE.

They could neither of 'em speak for rage and so fell a sputtering at one another like two roasting apples.   *Congreve.*

My rage is not malicious; like a spark
Of fire by steel inforced out of a flint.
It is no sooner kindled, but extinct.   *Goffe.*

RAIN.

How beautiful is the rain!
After the dust and heat,
In the broad and fiery street,
In the narrow lane;
How beautiful is the rain!
How it clatters along the roofs,
Like the tramp of hoofs;
How it gushes and struggles out
From the throat of the overflowing spout. *Longfellow.*

Dashing in big drops on the narrow pane,
   And making mournful music for the mind,
   While plays his interlude the wizard wind,
I hear the singing of the frequent rain. *Wm. H. Burleigh.*

RAINBOW.

How glorious is thy girdle cast,
   O'er mountain, tower, and town;

Or mirror'd in the ocean vast,
  A thousand fathoms down. *Campbell.*

That gracious thing, made up of tears and light. *Coleridge.*

What skillful limner e'er would choose
To paint the rainbow's various hues,
Unless to mortal it were given
To dip his brush in dyes of heaven? *Scott.*

RANK.

The rank is but the guinea's stamp
The man's the gowd for a' that. *Burns.*

RANT.

  Nay, an' thou 'lt mouth,
I'll rant as well as thou. *Shakespeare.*

RAPTURE.

Not the poet in the moment
Fancy lightens on his e'e,
Kens the pleasure, feels the rapture
That thy presence gi'es to me. *Burns.*

RASCALS.

Make yourself an honest man, and then you may be sure
that there is one rascal less in the world. *Carlyle.*

RASHNESS.

That's a valiant flea that dare eat his breakfast on the lip
of a lion. *Shakespeare.*

READING.

As a man may be eating all day, and for want of digestion
is never nourished, so these endless readers may cram themselves in vain with intellectual food. *Dr. I. Watts.*

Read not to contradict and confute, nor to believe and take
for granted, nor to find talk and discourse,—but to weigh and
consider. *Bacon.*

To read without reflecting, is like eating without digesting.

Burke.

REASON.

He who will not reason, is a bigot; he who cannot, is a fool; and he who dares not, is a slave.   *Byron.*

When a man has not a good reason for doing a thing, he has one good reason for letting it alone.   *Sir Walter Scott.*

One can never repeat too often, that reason, as it exists in man, is only our intellectual eye, and that, like the eye, to see, it needs light,—to see clearly and far, it needs the light of heaven.   *Anon.*

Reason is the test of ridicule—not riducle the test of truth.

Warburton.

Neither great poverty, nor great riches, will hear reason.

Fielding.

RECKONING.

I am ill at reckoning; it fits the spirit of a tapster.

Shakespeare.

So comes a reck'ning when the banquet's o'er,
The dreadful reck'ning and men smile no more.   *Gay.*

RECREATION.

Amusements to virtue are like breezes of air to the flame —gentle ones will fan it, but strong ones will put it out.

David Thomas.

REFINEMENT.

That only can with propriety be styled refinement which, by strengthening the intellect, purifies the manners.   *Coleridge.*

REFLECTION.

There is one art of which man should be master,—the art of reflection.   *Coleridge.*

REFORM.

Reform, like charity, must begin at home. Once well at home, how will it radiate outwards, irrepressible, into all that we touch and handle, speak and work; kindling every new light by incalculable contagion, spreading, in geometric ratio, far and wide, doing good only wherever it spreads, and not evil.

Carlyle.

He who reforms himself, has done more towards reforming the public, than a crowd of noisy, impotent patriots. *Lavater.*

REGULARITY.

Regularity is unity, unity is godlike, only the devil is changeable. *Richter.*

RELIGION.

Religion is the best armor that a man can have, but it is the worst cloak. *Bunyan.*

True religion
Is always mild, propitious, and humble
Plays not the tyrant, plants no faith in blood;
Nor bears destruction on her chariot-wheels;
But stoops to polish, succor, and redress,
And builds her grandeur on the public good. *Miller.*

Genuine religion is not so much a matter of feeling as of principle. *Anon.*

An atheist is but a mad ridiculous derider of piety; but a hypocrite makes a sober jest of God and religion; he finds it easier to be upon his knees than to rise to a good action.

Pope.

Men will wrangle for religion; write for it; fight for it; die for it; anything but—*live for it.* *Colton.*

Measure not men by Sundays, without regarding what they do all the week after. *Fuller.*

I have lived long enough to know what I did not at one time believe—that no society can be upheld in happiness and honor without the sentiment of religion.   *La Place.*

Pure religion and undefiled before God and the Father is this: To visit the fatherless and widows in their affliction, and to keep himself unspotted from the world.   *James* i, 27.

For in religion as in friendship, they who profess most are ever the least sincere.   *Sheridan.*

A man devoid of religion, is like a horse without a bridle.
From the Latin.

REMEMBRANCE.

Let never day nor night unhallow'd pass,
But still remember what the Lord has done.   *Shakespeare.*

REMORSE.

Remorse is the echo of a lost virtue.   *Bulwer Lytton.*

One of those terrible moments when the wheel of passion stands suddenly still.   *Bulwer Lytton.*

REPENTANCE.

Repentance,
A salve, a comfort, and a cordial;
He that hath her, the keys of heaven hath:
This is the guide, this is the post, the path.   *Drayton.*

REPOSE.

Our foster-nurse of nature is repose.   *Shakespeare.*

When a man finds not repose in himself it is in vain for him to seek it elsewhere.   *From the French.*

REPROOF.

Forbear sharp speeches to her; she's a lady,
So tender of rebukes that words are strokes,
And strokes death to her.   *Shakespeare.*

REPUTATION.

O reputation! dearer far than life,
Thou precious balsam, lovely, sweet of smell,
Whose cordial drops once spilt by some rash hand,
Not all the owner's care, nor the repenting toil
Of the rude spiller, ever can collect
To its first purity and native sweetness. *Sir W. Raleigh.*

How many people live on the reputation of the reputation
they might have made! *Holmes.*

How difficult it is to save the bark of reputation from the
rocks of ignorance. *Petrarch.*

Thy credit wary keep, 'tis quickly gone:
Being got by many actions, lost by one. *Randolph.*

The reputation of a man is like his shadow: It sometimes
follows and sometimes precedes him, it is sometimes longer
and sometimes shorter than his natural size. *French Proverb.*

RESIGNATION.

Whate'er my doom;
It cannot be unhappy: God hath given me
The boon of resignation. *Wilson.*

It is the Lord: let Him do what seemeth Him good.
Samuel iii, 18.

The Lord gave, and the Lord hath taken away; blessed
be the name of the Lord. *Job* i, 21..

REST.

Rest is the sweet sauce of labor. *Plutarch.*

Alternate rest and labor long endure. *Ovid.*

RETREAT.

In all the trade of war, no feat
Is nobler than a brave retreaat. *Butler.*

RETRIBUTION.

Man never fastened one end of a chain around the neck
of his brother, that God's own hand did not fasten the other end
round the neck of the oppressor.   *Lamartine.*

And thus the whirligig of time brings in his revenges.
Shakespeare.

REVENGE.

How rash, how inconsiderate is rage!
How wretched, oh! how fatal is our error,
When to revenge precipitate we run;
Revenge, that still with double force recoils
Back on itself, and is its own revenge,
While to the short liv'd, momentary joy,
Succeeds a train of woes, an age of torments.   *Frowde.*

The best sort of revenge is not to be like him who did the
injury.   *Antoninus.*

RHETORIC.

The heart's still rhetoric, disclosed with eyes.
Shakespeare.

RHYME AND REASON.

I was promised on a time,
To have reason for my rhyme;
From that time until this season,
I received no rhyme nor reason.   *Spenser.*

RICHES.

And his best riches, ignorance of wealth.   *Goldsmith.*

As riches and favor forsake a man, we discover him to be
a fool, but nobody could find it out in his prosperity.
La Bruyère.

He hath riches sufficient, who hath enough to be charitable.
Sir Thomas Browne.

A great fortune is a great slavery. *Seneca.*

Believe not much them that seem to despise riches; for they despise them that despair of them; and none are worse when they come to them. Be not penny-wise; riches have wings, and sometimes they fly away of themselves, sometimes they must be set flying to bring in more. *Bacon.*

Rich, not be exalted; poor, be not dejected. *Cleobulus.*

RIDICULE.

If ridicule were employed to laugh men out of vice and folly, it might be of some use; but it is made use of to laugh men out of virtue and good sense, by attacking everything solemn and serious. *Addison.*

RING.

Oh! how many torments lie in the small circle of a wedding ring. *Colley Cibber.*

RIVALRY.

Two stars keep not motion in one sphere. *Shakespeare.*

ROARING.

I will roar, that it will do any man's heart good to hear me. *Anon.*

I will aggravate my voice so, that I will roar you as gently as any sucking dove; I will roar you as 'twere any nightingale. *Shakespeare.*

ROD.

Take thy correction mildly. Kiss the rod. *Shakespeare.*

He that spareth his rod hateth his son. *Proverbs* xiii, 24.

RUDENESS.

A man has no more right to say an uncivil thing, than to act one; no more right to say a rude thing to another, than to knock him down. *Johnson.*

RUMOR.

The flying rumors gather'd as they roll'd
Scarce any tale was sooner heard than told
And all who told it added something new,
And all who heard it made enlargement, too,
In every ear it spread, on every tongue it grew. *Pope.*

SABBATH.

The poor man's day. *Grahame.*

The Sabbath was made for man, and not man for the Sabbath. *St. Mark* ii, 27.

SAILOR.

I love the sailor; his eventful life—
His generous spirit—his contempt of danger—
His firmness in the gale, the wreck, the strife;
And though a wild and reckless ocean-ranger,
God grant he make the port, when life is o'er,
Where storms are hush'd, and billows break no more.
Walter Colton.

SATAN.

Th' infernal serpent; he it was, whose guile,
Stirr'd up with envy and revenge, deceiv'd
The mother of mankind. *Milton.*

Here we may reign secure; and in my choice
To reign is worth ambition, though in hell.
Better to reign in hell than serve in heaven. *Milton.*

199

SATIETY.

A surfeit of the sweetest things,
The deepest loathing to the stomach brings.   *Shakespeare.*

SATIRE.

Wit larded with malice.   *Shakespeare.*

A bitter jest, when the satire comes too near the truth,
leaves a sharp sting behind.   *Tacitus.*

SCANDAL.

Nor do they trust their tongues alone,
But speak a language of their own;
Can read a nod, a shrug, a look,
Far better than a printed book;
Convey a libel in a frown,
And wink a reputation down;
Or, by the tossing of a fan,
Describe the lady and the man.   *Swift.*

SCAR.

A scar nobly got is a good livery of honor.   *Shakespeare.*

SCEPTICISM.

I would rather dwell in the dim fog of superstition than in
air rarified to nothing by the air pump of unbelief; in which
the panting breast expires, vainly and convulsively gasping for
breath.   *Richter.*

SCHEMES.

The best laid schemes o' mice an' men,
    Gang aft agley,
And lea'e us nought but grief and pain,
    For promised joy.   *Burns.*

SCORN.

Oh! what a thing, ye gods, is scorn or pity!
Heap on me, Heaven, the heat of all mankind,
Load me with envy, malice, detestation;
Let me be horrid to all apprehension;
Let the world shun me, so I 'scape but scorn.   *Lee.*

SCULPTURE.

A statue lies hid in a block of marble; and the art of the
statuary only clears away the superfluous matter, and removes
the rubbish.   *Addison.*

SEA.

Praise the sea, but keep on land.   *Geo. Herbert.*

SECRET.

'Tis in my memory lock'd,
And you yourself shall keep the key of it.   *Shakespeare.*

A secret in his mouth,
Is like a wild bird put into a cage;
Whose door no sooner opens, but 'tis out.   *Jonson.*

Generally he perceived in men of devout simplicity this
opinion; that the secrets of nature were the secrets of God,
part of that glory into which man is not to press too boldly.
        Bacon.

SELF.

And though all cry down self, none means
His ownself in a literal sense.   *Butler.*

Be always displeased with what thou art, if thou desirest
to attain to what thou art not; for where thou hast pleased thyself, there thou abidest. But if thou sayest I have enough, thou
perishest. Always add, always walk, always proceed. Neither
stand still, nor go back, nor deviate.   *Augustine.*

SELF-CONFIDENCE.

For they can conquer who believe they can.   *Virgil.*

SELF-CONTROL.

He who reigns within himself, and rules passions, desires and fears, is more than a king.   *Milton.*

SELF-DECEPTION.

No man was ever so much deceived by another as by himself.   *Greville.*

SELF-DEFENSE.

Self-defense is nature's eldest law.   *Dryden.*

SELF-HELP.

Help yourself, and Heaven will help you.   *La Fontaine.*

I have ever held it as a maxim, never to do that through another, which it was possible for me to execute myself.

Montesquieu.

SELF-LOVE.

Self-love is more cunning than the most cunning man in the world.   *La Rochefoucauld.*

Self-love is the greatest of flatterers.   *La Rochefoucauld.*

Of all mankind, each loves himself the best.   *Terence.*

SELF-RESPECT.

The reverence of a man's self is, next religion, the chiefest bridle of all vices.   *Lord Bacon.*

SENSE.

Something there is more needful than expense
And something previous e'en to taste—'tis sense:

Good sense which only is the gift of heaven,
And though no science, fairly worth the seven.   *Pope.*

SENSIBILITY.

The heart that is soonest awake to the flowers,
Is always the first to be touch'd by the thorns.   *Moore.*

SERVANT.

Master, go on, and I will follow thee
To the last gasp, with truth and loyalty.   *Shakespeare.*

If thou hast a loitering servant, send him of thy errand
just before his dinner.   *Fuller.*

SERVICES.

The daisy, by the shadow that it casts,
    Protects the ling'ring dewdrop from the sun.

    Wordsworth.

SHAME.

It is the guilt, not the scaffold, which constitutes the shame.
    Corneille.

SHAVING.

Men for their sins
Have shaving, too, entail'd upon their chins.   *Byron.*

SHIP.

She comes majestic with her swelling sails,
The gallant bark; along her watery way
Homeward she drives before the favoring gales;
Now flirting at their length the streamers play,
And now they ripple with the ruffling breeze.   *Southey.*

SILENCE.

The temple of our purest thoughts is—silence! *Mrs. Hale.*

Fellows who have no tongues are often all eyes and ears.
Haliburton.

Let us be silent, that we may hear the whispers of the gods.
Emerson.

SIMPLICITY.

Whose nature is so far from doing harm,
That he suspects none. *Shakespeare.*

SIN.

He that falls into sin is a man; that grieves at it may be a
saint; that boasteth of it is a devil. *Fuller.*

Few love to hear the sins they love to act. *Shakespeare.*

SINCERITY.

The more honesty a man has, the less he affects the air
of a saint. The affectation of sanctity is a blotch on the face
of piety. *Lavater.*

Sincerity is like traveling in a plain beaten road, which
commonly brings a man sooner to his journey's end than
byways, in which men often lose themselves. *Tillotson.*

SKULL

Where be your gibes now? your gambols? your songs?
your flashes of merriment that were wont to set the table on a
roar? *Shakespeare.*

SLANDER.
Slander—
Whose edge is sharper than the sword. *Shakespeare.*

Slander meets no regard from noble minds;
Only the base believe, what the base only utter. *Beller.*

SLANDERERS.

Long-breath'd, talkers, minion lispers,
Cutting honest throats by whispers.   *Scott.*

SLEEP.

Sleep, that knits up the ravell'd sleeve of care;
The death of each day's life, sore labor's bath,
Balm of hurt minds, great Nature's second course,
Chief nourisher in life's feast.   *Shakespeare.*

Downy sleep, death's counterfeit.   *Shakespeare.*

How wonderful is death, death and his brother, sleep!
                                                    Shelley.

O magic sleep! O comfortable bird,
That broodest o'er the troubled sea of the mind
Till it is hush'd and smooth! O unconfin'd
Restraint! imprison'd liberty! great key
To golden palaces—ay, all the world
Of silvery enchantment   *Keats.*

SNEER.

There was a laughing devil in his sneer,
That raised emotions both of rage and fear,
And where his frown of hatred darkly fell,
Hope, withering, fled, and mercy sighed farewell.   *Byron.*

A habit of sneering, marks the egotist, or the fool, or the
knave or all three.   *Lavater.*

SOCIETY.

Society is like a lawn where every roughness is smoothed,
every bramble eradicated, and where the eye is delighted by
the smiling verdure of a velvet surface. He, however, who
would study nature in its wildness and variety, must plunge into
the forest, must explore the glen, must stem the torrent, and
dare the precipice.   *Washington Irving.*

SOLITUDE.

Alone on a wide, wide sea,
So lonely 'twas, that God himself
Scarce seemed there to be.   *Coleridge.*

Oh, lost to virtue—lost to manly thought,
Lost to the noble sallies of the soul!
Who think it solitude to be alone.   *Young.*

The thought,
The deadly thought of solitude.   *Keats.*

SORROW.

When sorrows come, they come not single spies,
But in battalions!   *Shakespeare.*

Any mind that is capable of a *real sorrow* is capable of
good.   *Mrs. Stowe.*

Sorrow seems sent for our instruction, as we darken the
cages of birds when we would teach them to sing.   *Richter.*

The first sharp sorrow—ay, the breaking up
Of that deep fountain, ne'er to be seal'd
Till we with time close up the great account.
                                          Caroline Bowles.

SOUL.

Alas! while the body stands so broad and brawny, must the
soul lie blinded, dwarfed, stupefied, almost annihilated? Alas!
this was, too, a breath of God, bestowed in heaven, but on
earth never to be unfolded!   *Carlyle.*

There are souls which fall from heaven like flowers, but
ere they bloom are crushed under the foul tread of some brutal
hoof.   *Richter.*

SPEAKING.

Speak but little and well, if you would be esteemed as a
man of merit.   *Trench.*

SPEECH.

A sentence well couched takes both the sense and the understanding. I love not those cart-rope speeches that are longer than the memory of man can fathom.   *Feltham.*

SPITE.

Spite is a little word but it represents as strange a jumble of feelings and compound of discords, as any polysyllable in the language.   *Dickens.*

SPOON.

He must have a long spoon that must eat with the devil.
                    Shakespeare.

SPRING.

Wide flush the fields; the softening air is balm;
Echo the mountains round; the forest smiles;
And every sense and every heart is joy.   *Thomson.*

STARS.

There they stand,
Shining in order like a living hymn
Written in light.   *Willis.*

The stars hang bright above,
Silent, as if they watch'd the sleeping earth. *Coleridge.*

Those gold candles fix'd in heaven's air.   *Shakespeare.*

STOICISM.

To feel for none is the true social art
Of the world's stoics—men without a heart.   *Byron.*

STORY-TELLING.

I cannot tell how the truth may be;
I say the tale as 'twas said to me.   *Sir Walter Scott.*

STUDY.

Much study is a weariness of the flesh.

Ecclesiastes xii, 12.

SUCCESS.

'Tis not in mortals to command success;
But we'll do more, Sempronius.—We'll deserve it.

Addison.

It is success that colors all in life;
Success makes fools admir'd, makes villains honest,
All the proud virtue of this vaunting world
Fawns on success and power, howe'er acquired.

Thomson.

SUICIDE.

Child of despair, and suicide my name. *Savage.*

Self-murder, that infernal crime,
Which all the gods level their thunder at! *Fane.*

SUN.

The glorious lamp of heaven, the sun. *Herrick.*

Open the casement, and up with the sun!
His gallant journey has now begun,
Over the hills his chariot is roll'd.
Banner'd with glory and burnish'd with gold;
Over the hills he comes sublime,
Bridegroom of earth, and brother of time!

Martin F. Tupper.

SUNRISE.

And see—the sun himself! on wings
Of glory up the east he springs.
Angel of light! who from the time
Those heavens began their march sublime,

Hath first of all the starry choir
Trod in his Maker's steps of fire.   *Moore.*

SUNSET.

See the descending sun
Scatt'ring his beams about him as he sinks,
And gilding heaven above, and seas beneath,
With paint no mortal pencil can express.   *Hopkins.*

SUPERSTITION.

Superstition renders a man a fool, and scepticism makes
him mad.   *Fielding.*

SUSPENSE.

It is a miserable thing to live in suspense, it is the life of
the spider.   *Swift.*

SUSPICION.

It is hardly possible to suspect another without having in
one's self the seeds of baseness the party is accused of.
                                                Stanislaus.

SWEARING.

Swear not at all: neither by heaven; for it is God's throne:
nor by the earth; for it is his footstool: neither by Jerusalem;
for it is the city of the great king. Neither shalt thou swear by
thy head, because thou canst not make one hair white or black.
But let your communication be yea, yea; nay nay: for whatsoever is more than these cometh of evil.   *St. Matthew.*

TACT.

Never join with your friend when he abuses his horse or
his wife, unless the one is about to be sold, and the other to
be buried.   *Colton.*

TALENTS.

It seems that nature has concealed at the bottom of our minds, talents and abilities of which we are not aware. The passions alone have the privilege of bringing them to light, and of giving us sometimes view more certain and more perfect than art could possibly produce.   *La Rochefoucauld.*

TALKERS.

As empty vessels make the loudest sound, so they that have the least wit are the greatest babblers.   *Plato.*

Talkers are no good doers.   *Shakespeare.*

TALKING.

Words learned by rote a parrot may rehearse,
But talking is not always to converse;
Not more distinct from harmony divine,
The constant creaking of a country sign.   *Cowper.*

Does a man speak foolishly?—suffer him gladly, for you are wise. Does he speak erroneously?—stop such a man's mouth with sound words that cannot be gainsaid. Does he speak truly? —rejoice in the truth.   *Oliver Cromwell.*

TASTE.

May not taste be compared to that exquisite sense of the bee, which instantly discovers and extracts the quintessence of every flower, and disregards all the rest of it.   *Greville.*

TEA.

Tea! thou soft, thou sober sage, and venerable liquid:—thou female tongue-running, smile-smoothing, heart-opening, wink-tippling cordial, to whose glorious insipidity I owe the happiest moments of my life, let me fall prostrate!   *Colley Cibber.*

TEARS.

Beauty's tears are lovelier than her smile.   *Campbell.*

The safetyvalves of the heart, when too much pressure is laid on. *Albert Smith.*

The tears of penitents are the wine of angels.
St. Bernard.

TEMPER.

A sunny temper gilds the edges of life's blackest cloud.
Guthrie.

TEMPTATION.

He who has no mind to trade with the devil, should be so wise as to keep from his shop. *South.*

'Tis one thing to be tempted,
Another thing to fall. *Shakespeare.*

TESTIMONY AND ARGUMENT.

Testimony is like an arrow shot from a long bow; the force of it depends on the strength of the hand that draws it. Argument is like an arrow from a cross-bow, which has equal force though shot by a child. *Bacon.*

THINKERS.

There are very few original thinkers in the world; the greatest part of those who are called philosophers have adopted the opinions of some who went before them. *Dugald Stewart.*

THOUGHT.

There's too much abstract willing, purposing,
In this poor world. *We talk by aggregates.*
And think by systems, and being used to face
Our evils in statistics, are inclined
To cap them with unreal remedies.
Drawn out in haste on the other side the slate.
Elizabeth Barrett Browning.

Man is a thinking being, whether he will or no: all he can do is to turn his thoughts the best way. *Sir W. Temple.*

Thoughts are but dreams till their effects be tried.

Shakespeare.

Kindred objects kindred thoughts inspire,
As summer clouds flash forth electric fire. *Rogers.*

TIME.

Time is the chrysalis of eternity. *Richter.*

I never knew the old gentleman with the scythe and hour-glass bring anything but grey hairs, thin cheeks, and loss of teeth. *Dryden.*

All that time is lost which might be better employed.

Rousseau.

The inaudible and noiseless foot of time. *Shakespeare.*

Time is the old Justice, that examines all offenders.

Shakespeare.

Who shall contend with time, unvanquished time,
The conqueror of conquerors, and lord of desolation?

Kirk White.

Still on it creeps,
Each little moment at another's heels,
Till hours, days, years, and ages are made up
Of such small parts as these, and men look back
Worn and bewildered, wondering how it is.
Thou trav'llest like a ship in the wide ocean,
Which hath no bounding shore to mark its progress.

Joanna Baillie.

As every thread of gold is valuable, so is every minute of time. *Mason.*

Dost thou love life? Then waste not time, for time is the stuff that life is made of. *B. Franklin.*

Time, as he passes us, has a dove's wing,
Unsoil'd and swift, and of a silken sound. *Cowper.*

TITLE.

A fool, indeed, has great need of a title,
It teaches men to call him count and duke,
And to forget his proper name of fool.   *Crowne.*

TO-DAY.

To-day is ours: why do we fear?
To-day is ours: we have it here;
Let's banish bus'ness, banish sorrow:
To the gods belongs to-morrow.   *Cowley.*

TO-MORROW.

To-morrow cheats us all. Why dost thou stay,
And leave undone what should be done to-day?
Begin—the present minute's in thy power;
But still t' adjourn, and wait a fitter hour,
Is like the clown, who at some river's side
Expecting stands, in hopes the running tide
Will all ere long be past. Fool! not to know
It still has flow'd the same, and will forever flow.   *Hughes.*

TONGUE.

The tongue the ambassador of the heart.   *Lyly.*

Restrain thy mind, and let mildness ever attend thy tongue.
          Theognis.

To many men well-fitting doors are not set on their tongues.
          Theognis.

TOOTHACHE.

There was never yet philosopher
That could endure the toothache patiently.   *Shakespeare.*

TREASON.

Treason doth never prosper. What's the reason?
Why, when it prospers, none dare call it treason.
          Sir John Harrington.

TRIFLES.

Those who bestow too much application on trifling things, become generally incapable of great ones. *La Rochefoucauld.*

TRUTH.

Truth is God's daughter. *Spanish Proverb.*

He who conceals a useful truth is equally guilty with the propagator of an injurious falsehood. *Augustine.*

"Truth," I cried, "though the heavens crush me for following her; no falsehood, though a whole celestial Lubberland were the price of apostacy!" *Carlyle.*

Truth is a gem that is found at a great depth; whilst on the surface of this world, all things are weighed by the false scale of custom. *Byron.*

There are three parts in truth: first, the inquiry, which is the wooing of it; secondly, the knowledge of it, which is the presence of it; and thirdly, the belief, which is the enjoyment of it. *Bacon.*

Truth needs no flowers of speech. *Pope.*

TWILIGHT.

How fine to view the sun's departing ray
Fling back a lingering lovely after-day;
The moon of summer glides serenely by,
And sheds a light enchantment o'er the sky.
These, sweetly mingling, pour upon the sight
A pencill'd shadowing, and a dewy light—
A softened day, a half-unconscious night.
Alas! too finely pure on earth to stay,
It faintly spots the hill, and dies away. *Anon.*

TYRANTS.

It is worthy of observation, that the most imperious masters over their own servants, are at the same time, the most abject slaves to the servants of other masters. *Seneca.*

UNCERTAINTY.

How happy could I be with either,
Were t'other dear charmer away.   *John Gay.*

UNKINDNESS.

Sharp-tooth'd unkindess.   *Shakespeare.*

UNWORTHINESS.

You are not worth the dust which the rude wind blows in
your face.   *Shakespeare.*

URGENCY.

The affair cries—haste,
And speed must answer it.   *Shakespeare.*

USURER.

A money-lender. He serves you in the present tense; he
lends you in the conditional mood; keeps you in the subjunc-
tive; and ruins you in the future!   *Addison.*

UTILITY.

Crab apples may not be the best kind of fruit; but a tree
which every year bears a great crop of crab apples is better
worth cultivating than a tree which bears nothing.

VALOR.

The better part of valor is discretion; in the which better
part I have saved my life.   *Shakespeare.*

The truly valiant dare everything but doing anybody an
injury.   *Sir Philip Sidney.*

VANITY.

She neglects her heart who studies her glass.   *Lavater.*

In a vain man, the smallest spark may kindle into the greatest flame, because the materials are always prepared for it. *Hume.*

Every man has just as much vanity as he wants understanding. *Pope.*

VANITY AND PRIDE.

Pride makes us esteem ourselves; vanity makes us desire the esteem of others. It is just to say, as Dean Swift has done, that a man is too proud to be vain. *Blair.*

VARIETY.

Variety's the very spice of life,
That gives it all its flavor. *Cowper.*

VERBIAGE.

Words, words, mere words, no matter from the heart.
Shakespeare.

VICE.

Vice repeated like the wandering wind,
Bows dust in others' eyes. *Shakespeare.*

Ah, vice! how soft are thy voluptuous ways,
While boyish blood is mantling, who can 'scape
The fascination of thy magic gaze?
A cherub-hydra round us dost thou gape,
And mould to every taste thy dear delusive shape. *Byron.*

Vice is a monster of so frightful mien,
As to be hated needs but to be seen;
Yet seen too oft, familiar with her face,
We first endure, then pity, then embrace. *Pope.*

Our pleasant vices
Are made the whip to scourage us. *Shakespeare.*

Vice stings us even in our pleasures, but virtue consoles us, even in our pains. *Colton.*

VICISSITUDES.

Thus doth the ever-changing course of things
Run a perpetual circle, ever turning;
And that same day, that highest glory brings,
Brings us unto the point of back-returning.   *Daniel.*

VIGILANCE.

The master's eye makes the horse fat.   *From the Latin.*

VILLAINY.

    The evil you teach us, we will execute, and it shall go hard
but we will better the instruction.   *Shakespeare.*

    He hath out-villained villainy so far, that the rarity redeems
him.   *Shakespeare.*

VIRTUE.

The only amaranthine flow'r on earth
Is virtue; the only lasting treasure, truth.   *Cowper.*

A heart unspotted is not easily daunted.   *Shakespeare.*

And virtue is her own reward.   *Prior.*

VITUPERATION.

The bitter clamor of two eager tongues.   *Shakespeare.*

VOCATION.

Why, Hal, 'tis my vocation.
'Tis no sin for a man to labor in his vocation.

Shakespeare.

VOICE.

Her voice was ever soft,
Gentle, and low; an excellent thing in woman.

Shakespeare.

VULGAR.

To endeavor to work upon the vulgar with fine sense, is like attempting to hew blocks with a razor. *Pope.*

WAGERS.

I've heard old cunning stagers
Say fools for arguments use wagers. *Butler.*

WANT.

His wit being snuft by want burnt clear. *Killigrew.*

WANTS.

The fewer our wants the nearer we resemble the gods.
Socrates.

Where necessity ends, curiosity begins; and no sooner are we supplied with every thing that nature can demand, than we sit down to contrive artificial appetites. *Johnson.*

WAR.

O war! begot in pride and luxury,
The child of malice and revengeful hate;
Thou impious good, and good impiety!
Thou art the foul refiner of a state,
Unjust scourge of men's iniquity,
Sharp easer of corruptions desperate!
Is there no means but that a sin-sick land
Must be let blood with such a boist'rous hand? *Daniels.*

Give me the money that has been spent in war, and I will purchase every foot of land upon the globe. I will clothe every man, woman and child in an attire of which kings and queens would be proud. I will build a school house on every hillside, and in every valley over the whole earth; I will build an academy in every town, and endow it; a college in every State, and fill it with able professors; I will crown every hill with a place of worship, consecrated to the promulgation of the gospel of peace; I will support in every pulpit an able teacher of righteousness, so that on every Sabbath morning the chime on one hill should answer to the chime on another round the earth's wide circumference; and the voice of prayer, and the song of praise, should ascend like an universal holocaust to heaven.

Henry Richard.

That mad game the world so loves to play. *Swift.*

> War, my lord,
> Is of eternal use to human kind,
> For ever and anon when you have pass'd
> A few dull years in peace and propagation
> The world is overstock'd with fools, and wants
> A pestilence at least if not a hero. *Jeffrey.*

WARRIORS.

If Europe should ever be ruined, it will be by its warriors.

Montesquieu.

WASTE.

What maintains one vice, would bring up two children. Remember, many a little makes a mickle: and farther, beware of little expenses; a small leak will sink a great ship.

Franklin.

WATER.

Traverse the desert, and then ye can tell
What treasures exist in the cold deep well,
Sink in despair on the red parch'd earth,
And then ye may reckon what water is worth.

Miss Eliza Cook.

WEALTH.

It is far more easy to acquire a fortune like a knave than to expend it like a gentleman. *Colton.*

The way to wealth is as plain as the way to market. It depends chiefly on two words, industry and frugality; that is, waste neither time nor money, but make the best use of both. Without industry and frugality nothing will do, and with them everything.   *Franklin.*

WICKEDNESS.

Wickedness may prosper for awhile, but at the long run, he that sets all knaves at work will pay them.   *L'Estrange.*

WIFE.

What is there in the vale of life
Half so delightful as a wife;
When friendship, love, and peace combine
To stamp the marriage-bond divine?   *Cowper.*

All other goods by Fortune's hand are given,
A wife is the peculiar gift of heaven.   *Pope.*

She who ne'er answers till her husband cools;
Or, if she rules him, never shows she rules;
Charms by accepting, by submitting sways,
Yet has her humor most when she obeys.   *Pope.*

WILL.

In idle wishes fools supinely stay,
Be there a will,—and wisdom finds a way.   *George Crabb.*

WILLS.

What you leave at your death, let it be without controversy, else the lawyers will be your heirs.   *Osborne.*

WIND.

The wind has a language, I would I could learn!
Sometimes 'tis soothing, and sometimes 'tis stern,
Sometimes it comes like a low sweet song,
And all things grow calm, as the sound floats along,

And the forest is lull'd by the dreamy strain,
And slumber sinks down on the wandering main,
And its crystal arms are folded in rest,
And the tall ship sleeps on its heaving breast.

L. E. Landon.

WINE.

Wine is a turncoat; first a friend, and then an enemy.

Fielding.

WISDOM.

Common sense in an uncommon degree is what the world calls wisdom. *Coleridge.*

It is far easier to be wise for others than to be so for one-self. *La Rochefoucauld.*

Call him wise whose actions, words and steps are all a clear *because* to a clear *why*. *Lavater.*

The wisest man is generally he who thinks himself the least so. *Boileau.*

WISHES.

What ardently we wish we soon believe. *Young.*

WIT.

Wit and judgment often are at strife,
Though meant to be each other's aid like man and wife.

Pope.

True wit is nature to advantage drest,
What oft was thought, but ne'er so well exprest,
Something whose truth, convinc'd at sight we find,
That gives us back the image of our mind. *Pope.*

WOMAN.

'Tis beauty that doth oft make women proud;

'Tis virtue, that doth make them most admired;
'Tis modesty, that makes them seem divine.   *Shakespeare.*

If the heart of a man is depress'd with cares,
The mist is dispelled when a woman appears.   *Gay.*

Ould nature swears, the lovely dears
  Her noblest work she classes, O;
Her 'prentice han' she tried on man,
  An' then she made the lasses, O.   *Burns.*

Woman is something between a flower and an angel,
First, then, a woman will or won't,—depend on't;
If she will do't, she will; and there's an end on't,
But, if she won't, since safe and sound your trust is,
Fear is affront; and jealousy injustice.   *Aaron Hill.*

O woman! lovely woman! nature made thee
To temper man: we had been brutes without you!

Otway.

Women have more strength in their looks than we have in
our laws, and more power by their tears than we have by our
arguments.   *Saville.*

O woman, in our hours of ease,
Uncertain, coy, and hard to please,
And variable as the shade
By the light quivering aspen made;
When pain and anguish wring the brow
A ministering angel thou!   *Scott.*

Woman's natural mission is to love, to love but one, to
love always.   *Michelet.*

Woman knows that the better she obeys the surer she is
to rule.   *Michelet.*

Woman's happiness is in obeying. She objects to men who
abdicate too much.   *Michelet.*

Disguise our bondage as we will,
'Tis woman, woman rules us still.   *Tom Moore.*

What manly eloquence could produce such an effect as
woman's silence.   *Michelet.*

222

He's a fool, who thinks by force, or skill,
To turn the current of a woman's will.   *Tuke.*

WORDS.

Words are men's daughters, but God's son are things.
                                              Johnson.

If you would be pungent, be brief; for it is with words as
with sunbeams—the more they are condensed the deeper they
burn.   *Southey.*

He that uses many words for the explaining any subject,
doth like the cuttlefish, hide himself for the most part in his own
ink.   *Ray.*

Words are things; and a small drop of ink,
Falling like dew upon a thought, produces
That which makes thousands, perhaps millions, think.

                                              Byron.

    Apt words have power to 'suage
The tumults of a troubled mind
And are as balm to fester'd wounds.   *Milton.*

WORKING AND TALKING.

By work you get money, by talk you get knowledge.
                                            Haliburton.

WORLD.

O what a glory doth this world put on,
For him who with fervent heart goes forth,
Under the bright and glorious sky and looks
On duties well performed, and days well spent.

                                            Longfellow.

Ay beauteous is the world, and many a joy
Floats through its wide dominion. But, alas,
When we would seize the winged good, it flies,
And step by step, along the path of life,
Allures our yearning spirits to the grave.   *Goethe.*

The world's a wood, in which all lose their way,
Though by a different path each goes astray.

Buckingham.

WORTH.

For what is worth in anything,
But so much money as 'twill bring?   *Butler.*

Worth makes the man, and want of it the fellow;
The rest is all but leather or prunella.   *Pope.*

WRITERS.

Every great or original writer in proportion as he is great
or original, must himself create the taste by which he must be
relished.   *Wordsworth.*

WRITING.

The world agrees
That he writes well who writes with ease.   *Prior.*

You write with ease to show your breeding
But easy writing's curst hard reading.   *Sheridan.*

To write well is at once to think well, to feel rightly, and
to render properly! it is to have, at the same time, mind, soul,
taste.   *Buffon.*

YEARS.

Winged time glides on insensibly, and deceives us; and
there is nothing more fleeting than years.   *Ovid.*

YOUTH.

What is youth?—a dancing billow,
Winds behind and rocks before.   *Moore.*

Crabbed age and youth

Cannot live together;
Youth is full of pleasure,
Age is full of care;
Youth like summer morn,
Age like winter weather;
Youth like summer brave,
Age like winter bare;
Youth is full of sport,
Age's breath is short;
Youth is nimble, age is lame;
Youth is hot and bold,
Age is weak and cold;
Youth is wild and age is tame,
Age, I do abhor thee;
Youth, I do adore thee;
 O, my love, my love is young.
Age, I do defy thee.
O sweet shepherd, hie thee,
For methinks thou stay'st too long.   *Shakespeare.*

ZEAL.

No wild enthusiast ever yet could rest
Till half mankind were like himself possessed. *Cowper.*

FAMOUS LINES FROM FAVORITE AUTHORS

SHAKESPEARE.

A little more than kin, and less than kind.

Seems, madam; nay it is; I know not seems.

Frailty, thy name is woman.
Like Niobe, all tears.

O that this too, too solid flesh would melt.

Springes to catch woodcocks.

When shall we three meet again,
In thunder, lightning, or in rain?
When the hurly-burly's done,

When the battle's lost and won.

Come what come may,
Time and the hour run through the longest day.

Your face, my Thane, is as a book, where men
May read strange matters.

Letting *I dare not* wait upon *I would*.
Like the poor cat i' the adage.

I dare do all that may become a man;
Who does more, is none.

We have scotched the snake, not killed it.

Infirm of purpose!
Thou canst not say I did it; never shake
Thy gory locks at me.

Double, double, toil and trouble.

Lay on, Macduff,
And damned be he that first cries. "Hold, enough!"

One fire burns out another's burning,
One pain is lessen'd by another's anguish.

For you and I are past our dancing days.

He jests at scars that never felt a wound.

Too early seen unknown, and known too late.

Parting is such sweet sorrow.

I am the very pink of courtesy.

Adversity's sweet milk, philosophy.

Eyes, look your last;
Arms, take your last embrace.
We have seen better days.

Beware the Ides of March.

But, for mine own part, it was Greek to me.

Cowards die many times before their death,
The valiant never taste of death but once.

Though last, not least in love.

If you have tears prepare to shed them now.

This was the most unkindest cut of all.

A friend should bear his friend's infirmities,
But Brutus makes mine greater than they are.

This was the noblest Roman of them all.

I am no orator as Brutus is,
.   .   .   I only speak right on.

One touch of nature makes the whole world kin.

So wise so young, they say, do ne'er live long.

A horse! a horse! my kingdom for a horse!

Misery acquaints a man with strange bedfellows.

He that dies pays all debts.

This is the long and short of it.

The King's English.

How use doth breed a habit in a man!

Condemn the fault, and not the actor of it.

What's mine is yours, and what is yours is mine.

Benedick the married man.

Sets the wind in that corner?

O, what men dare do! what men may do! what men daily
do, not knowing what they do!

Are you good men and true?

Done to death by slanderous tongues.

My cake is dough

There's small choice in rotten apples.

In maiden meditation, fancy free.

My heart
  Is true as steel.
    Gives to airy nothing
A local habitation and a name.

A bright particular star.

The inaudible and noiseless foot of time.

Life is as tedious as a twice-told tale,
Vexing the dull ear of a dreaming man.

Midsummer madness.

Still you keep o' the windy side o' the law.

I like not fair terms and a villain's mind.

'Tis vile, unless it may be quaintly order'd,
And better, in my mind, not undertook.

Who chooseth me shall gain what many men desire.

Who chooseth me shall get as much as he deserves.

Who chooseth me must give or hazard all he hath.

I will assume desert.

O, these deliberate fools, when they do choose,
They have the wisdom by their wit to lose.

What, wouldst thou have a serpent sting thee twice?

    A Daniel come to judgment!
            O wise and upright judge,
How much more elder art thou than thy looks!

Is it so nominated in the bond?

I cannot find it; 'tis not in the bond.

A Daniel, still say I, a second Daniel!
I thank thee, Jew, for teaching me that word.

He is well paid that is well satisfied. Sir, you are very welcome to our house; It must appear in other ways than words,
Therefore I scant this breathing courtesy.

Motley's the only wear.

I had rather have a fool to make me merry, than experience to make me sad.

The Retort Courteous.—The Lie Circumstantial.—The Lie Direct.

Good wine needs no bush.

Your *If* is the only peacemaker; much virtue in *If*.

The ripest fruit first falls.

He will give the devil his due.

I know a trick worth two of that.

It would be argument for a week, laughter for a month, and a good jest forever.

Brain him with a lady's fan.

A good mouth-filling oath.

Shall I not take mine ease in mine inn?

I could have better spared a better man.

He hath eaten me out of house and home.

Uneasy lies the head that wears a crown.

Thy wish was father, Harry, to that thought.

How sharper than a serpent's tooth it is
To have a thankless child!

Striving to better, oft we mar what's well.

I am a man
More sinned against than sinning.

O, that way madness lies; let me shun that.

The little dogs and all,
Tray, Blanche, and Sweetheart, see, they bark at me.

Ay, every inch a king.

But I will wear my heart upon my sleeve

For daws to peck at.

Put money in thy purse.

Framed to make women false.

For I am nothing, if not critical.

Iago.—What, are you hurt, lieutenant?

Cas.—Ay, past all surgery.

O thou invisible spirit of wine, if thou hast no name to be known by, let us call thee devil!

O that men should put an enemy in their mouths to steal away their brains!

Trifles, light as air,
Are to the jealous confirmations strong
As proofs of holy writ.

Speak of me as I am; nothing extenuate.
Nor set down aught in malice; then must you speak
Of one that lov'd, not wisely, but too well.

My salad days,
When I was green in judgment.
It beggared all description.

Age cannot wither her, nor custom stale
Her infinite variety.

Let's do it after the high Roman fashion.

As it fell upon a day
In the merry month of May.

We are such stuff
As dreams are made on, and our little life
Is rounded with a sleep.

JONATHAN SWIFT.

Bread is the staff of life.

No wise man ever wished to be younger.

I shall be like that tree; I shall die at the top.

EDWARD YOUNG.

At thirty man suspects himself a fool;
Knows it at forty and reforms his plan.
      Be wise with speed;
A fool at forty is a fool indeed.

How blessings brighten as they take their flight.

Wishing, of all employments, is the worst.

And all may do what has by man been done.

          Beautiful as sweet!
And young as beautiful! and soft as young
And gay as soft! and innocent as gay.
  'Tis impious in a good man to be sad.

JOHN DRYDEN.

None but the brave deserve the fair.

And like another Helen, fired another Troy.

Who think too little, and who talk too much.

Everything by starts, and nothing long.

The young men's vision, and the old men's dream.

She hugged the offender and forgave the offense.

Sex to the last.

For Art may err, but Nature cannot miss.

Errors, like straws, upon the surface flow;
He who would search for pearls must dive below.

All delays are dangerous in war.

ALEXANDER POPE.

Thou wert my guide, philosopher, and friend.

'Tis education forms the common mind:
Just as the twig is bent the tree's inclined.

Odious in woolen! 'twould a saint provoke!

Who shall decide when doctors disagree,
And soundest causists doubt, like you and me?

Heaven from all creatures hides the book of fate.

Shoot folly as it flies.

Lo, the poor Indian! whose untutored mind
Sees God in clouds. or hears Him in the wind.

Honor and shame from no condition rise;
Act well your part, there all the honor lies.

Curst be the verse, how well soe'er it flow,
That tends to make one worthy man my foe.

There St. John mingles with my friendly bowl,
The feast of reason, and the flow of soul.

Welcome the coming, speed the departing guest.

The last and greatest art, the art to blot.

I am his Highness' dog at Kew,
Pray tell me, sir, whose dog are you?

Thou great First Cause, least understood.

Whatever is. is right.

JOHN MILTON.

Tears, such as angels weep, burst forth.

Which, if not victory, is yet revenge.

The bright consummate flower.

Deep-versed in books and shallow in himself.

When more is meant than meets the ear.

The oracles are dumb.

That old man eloquent.

License they mean when they cry liberty.

JOSEPH ADDISON.

My voice is still for war,
Gods! can a Roman senate long debate
Which of the two to choose. slavery or death?

A day, an hour, of virtuous liberty
Is worth a whole eternity in bondage.

The woman who deliberates is lost.

The spacious firmament on high,
With all the blue ethereal sky—

.　　　.　　　.　　　.

Forever singing, as they shine,
The hand that made us is divine.

EDMUND BURKE.

There is, however, a limit at which forbearance ceases to
be a virtue.

But the age of chivalry is gone. That of sophisters, econo-
mists, and calculators has succeeded.

Early and provident fear is the mother of safety.

WILLIAM COWPER.

England, with all thy faults, I love thee still,
My country!

She that asks
Her dear five hundred friends.

The beggarly last doit.

A fool must now and then be right by chance.

A hat not much the worse for wear.

And Satan trembles when he sees
The weakest saint upon his knees.

Beware of desperate steps. The darkest day,
Live till to-morrow, will have passed away.

233

OLIVER GOLDSMITH.

And learn the luxury of doing good.

These little things are great to little man.

But winter lingering, chills the lap of May.

He cast off his friends, as a huntsman his pack,
For he knew, when he choosed, he could whistle them
back.

SAMUEL TAYLOR COLERIDGE.

As idle as a painted ship
Upon a painted ocean.

Water, water, everywhere,
Nor any drop to drink.

A sadder and a wiser man
He rose the morrow morn.

He prayeth best, who loveth best
All things, both great and small.

A sight to dream of, not to tell.

Alas! they had been friends in youth;
But whispering tongues can poison truth;
And constancy lives in realms above;
    And life is thorny, and youth is vain,
And to be wroth with one we love,
    Doth work like madness in the brain.

Motionless torrents! silent cataracts!
Ye living flowers that skirt the eternal frost.

Our myriad-minded Shakespeare.

A dwarf sees farther than the giant when he has the giant's
shoulder to mount on.

THOMAS CAMPBELL.

'Tis distance lends enchantment to the view.
And robes the mountain in its azure hue.

The combat deepens. On, ye brave,
Who rush to glory or the grave!

To bear is to conquer our fate.

LORD BYRON.

'Tis pleasant, sure, to see one's name in print;
A book's a book, although there's nothing in't.

With just enough of learning to misquote.

Maid of Athens, ere we part.
Give, oh! give me back my heart.

Had sighed to many, though he loved but one.

The dome of Thought, the palace of the Soul.

Hereditary bondsmen! know ye not,
Who would be free, themselves must strike the blow.

   Music arose with its voluptuous swell—
Soft eyes looked love to eyes which spake again.
   And all went merry as a marriage bell.

On with the dance! let joy be unconfined.

And there was mounting in hot haste.

I stood in Venice, on the Bridge of Sighs;
A palace and a prison on each hand.

Man!
Thou pendulum betwixt a smile and tear.
"While stands the Coliseum Rome shall stand;
When falls the Coliseum, Rome shall fall;
And when Rome falls—the world."

I die—but first I have possess'd,
And come what may, I have been blest.

He makes a solitude, and calls it—peace.

Hark! to the hurried question of despair,
"Where is my child?"—an Echo answers
   —"Where?"

The power of Thought—the magic of the mind.

And both were young, and one was beautiful.

A change came o'er the spirit of my dream.

My boat is on the shore
And my bark is on the sea.

The precious porcelain of common clay.

Society is now one polished horde.
Formed of two mighty tribes, the Bores, and Bored.

I awoke one morning and found myself famous.

The best of Prophets of the future is the past.

   And what is writ, is writ—
Would it were worthier?

JOHN KEATS.

Philosophy will clip an angel's wings.

Thou foster-child of Silence and slow Time.

TALLEYRAND.

Prudence in women should be an instinct, not a virtue.

What I have been taught I have forgotten; what I know
I have guessed.

The love of glory can only create a hero: the contempt of
it creates a great man.

If you wish to appear agreeable in society, you must con-
sent to be taught many things which you know already.

There are two things to which we never grow accustomed—
the ravages of time and the injustice of our fellow-men.

He who cannot feel friendship is alike incapable of love.
Let a woman beware of the man who owns that he loves no one
but herself.

It is sometimes quite enough for a man to feign ignorance

of that which he knows, to gain the reputation of knowing that of which he is ignorant.

Human life is like a game of chess—each piece holds its place upon the chessboard—king, queen, bishop, and pawn. Death comes, the game is up, and all are thrown, without distinction, pell-mell in the same bag.

CHARLES DICKENS.

In a Pickwickian sense.

When found, make a note of.

My life is one demd horrid grind.

Barkis is willin'.

Lor! let's be comfortable.

In came Mrs. Fezziweg, one vast substantial smile.

Oh, a dainty plant is the ivy green,
　　That creepeth o'er ruins old!
Of right choice foods are his meals, I ween,
　　In his cell so lone and cold.
Creeping where no life is seen, . . .
A rare old plant is the ivy green.

MISCELLANEOUS QUOTATIONS.

Build thee more stately mansions, O my soul,
　　As the swift seasons roll!
　　Leave thy low vaulted past!
Let each new temple, nobler than the last,
Shut three from heaven with a dome more vast,
　　Till thou at length art free,
Leaving thine outgrown shell by life's unresting sea!
　　　　　　　　　　　　O. W. Holmes.

For myself alone I doubt;
All is well, I know, without;
I alone the beauty mar,
I alone the music jar.

Yet with hands by evil stained,
And an ear by discord pained,
I am groping for the keys
Of the heavenly harmonies.   *J. G. Whittier.*

Into the sunshine,
  Full of the light,
Leaping and flashing
  From morn till night!

.   .   .   .

Glorious fountain!
  Let my heart be
Fresh, changeful, constant,
  Upward, like thee!   *J. R. Lowell.*

I knew a very wise man that believed that if a man were
permitted to make all the ballads he need not care who should
make the laws of a nation.   *Andrew Fletcher.*

Then gently scan your brother man,
  Still gentler, sister woman;
Though they may gang a kennin wrang,
  To step aside is human.

.   .   .   .

What's done we partly may compute,
But know not what's resisted . .   *Burns.*

  Alas for the rarity
Of Christian charity
  Under the sun!   *Thomas Hood.*

Like the dew on the mountain,
  Like the foam on the river,
Like the bubble on the fountain,
  Thou art gone, and forever!   *Scott.*

Philosophy is the romance of the aged, and Religion the
only future history for us all.   *Balbi.*

Boston State House is the hub of the Solar System. You
couldn't pry that out of a Boston man if you had the tire of
all creation straightened out for a crowbar.

                                            O. W. Holmes.

Say—the world is a nettle; disturb it, it stings:
Grasp it firmly, it stings not. On one of two things,
If you would not be stung, it behooves you to settle;
Avoid it, or crush it.   *Owen Meredith.*

Tender-handed grasp a nettel
  And it stings you for your pains;
Grasp it like a man of mettle
  And it soft as silk remains.   *Aaron Hill.*

Every man has in himself a continent of undiscovered
character. Happy he who acts the Columbus to his own soul!
                                              Stephen.

Conquering, not as anger is cowed by fiercer anger, or hate
by bitterer hate, but as anger is subdued by patience and hatred is conquered by love. And the conquests of patience and
love are slow.
                 Author of Schonberg-Cotta Family.

O noble conscience, upright and refined,
How slight a fault inflicts a bitter sting.
                          Daniel Webster.

Nature fits all her children with something to do
He who would write and can't write, can surely review.
                               J. R. Lowell.

Meanwhile the guilty soul cannot keep its own secret. It is
false to itself; or rather, it feels an irresistible impulse of conscience to be true to itself. . . . It must be confessed—it *will* be
confessed—there is no refuge from confession but suicide, and
suicide is confession.
                             Daniel Webster.

How sink the brave who sink to rest,
By all their country's wishes blest!

  .   .   .   .

By fairy hands their knell is rung;
There Honor comes, a pilgrim gray,
To bless the turf that wraps their clay;
And Freedom shall awhile repair,
To dwell a weeping hermit there.   *Collins.*

Was it something said,
  Something done.
Vexed him? was it touch of hand,
  Turn of head?
Strange! that very way
  Love began.
I as little understand
  Love's decay.   *Robert   Browning.*

The mossy marbles rest
On the lips that he has prest
  In their bloom:
And the names he loved to hear
Have been carved for many a year
  On the tomb.   *O. W. Holmes.*

We may live without poetry, music, and art;
We may live without conscience, and live without heart;
We may live without friends; we may live without books;
But civilized man cannot live without cooks.
He may live without books—what is knowledge but grieving?
He may live without hope—what is hope but deceiving?
He may live without love—what is passion but pining?
But where is the man that can live without dining?
                                   Owen Meredith.

Not a dram was heard, not a funeral note.
As his corpse to the rampart we hurried.

    .   .   .   .

But he lay like a warrior taking his rest,
With his martial cloak around him.

    .   .   .

We carved not a line, and we raised not a stone,
But we left him alone in his glory.
                                   Charles Wolfe.

    The consciousness of clean linen is in and of itself a source
of moral strength only second to that of a clean conscience. A
well-ironed collar, or a fresh glove, has carried many a man
through the emergency in which a wrinkle or a rip would have
defeated him.   *E. S. Phelps.*

    Grant me, O sweet and loving Jesus, to rest in Thee, above all other creatures, above all health and beauty, above all glory and honour, above all power and dignity, above all knowledge and subtlety, above all riches and arts, above all joy and gladness, above all fame and praise, above all sweetness and comfort, above all hope and promise, above all desert and desire, above all gifts and benefits that Thou canst give and impart unto us, above all mirth and joy that the mind of man can receive and feel; finally, above angels and archangels, and above all the heavenly host, above all things visible and invisible, and above all that Thou art not, O my God.

Thomas à Kempis.

Within that awful volume lies
The mystery of mysteries!

.   .   .   .

And better had they ne'er been born,
Who read to doubt, or read to scorn.   *Scott.*

The paths of glory lead but to the grave.   *Gray's Elegy.*

A dull mind, once arriving at an inference that flatters a desire, is rarely able to retain the impression that the notion from which the inference started was purely problematical.

George Eliot.

Sometimes, I think, the things we see
Are shadows of the things to be:
    That what we plan we build;
That every hope that hath been crossed,
And every dream we thought was lost,
    In Heaven shall be fulfilled.   *Phoebe Cary.*

Life! we've been long together,
Through pleasant and through cloudy weather;
    'Tis hard to part when friends are dear;
    Perhaps 'twill cost a sigh, a tear.
Then steal away, give little warning,
    Choose thine own time:
Say not "Good night," but in some brighter clime
    Bid me "Good morning."   *Mrs. Barbauld.*

The love of Ophelia. which she never once confesses, is like a secret which we have stolen from her, and which ought to die upon our hearts as upon her own.   *Mrs. Jamison.*

When love and skill work together, expect a masterpiece.
Charles Reade.

Love feels no burden, thinks nothing of trouble, attempts what is above its strength, pleads no excuse of impossibility; for it thinks all things lawful for itself. and all things possible.

It is therefore able to undertake all things, and it completes many things, and brings them to a conclusion, where he who does not love, faints and lies down.   *Thomas à Kempis.*

> Shall I, wasting in despair,
> Die because a woman's fair?
> Or make pale my cheeks with care,
> 'Cause another's rosy are?
>
> Be she fairer than the day,
> Or the flowery meads in May,
> If she be not so to me,
> What care I how fair she be?   *George Wither.*

> I could not love thee, dear, so much,
> Loved I not honor more.   *Richard Lovelace.*

Where true love has found a home, every new year forms one more ring around the hearts of those who love each other, so that in the end they cannot live apart.   *Julius Stinde.*

Fain would I climb, yet fear I to fall.   *Sir Walter Raleigh.*

If thy heart fails thee, climb not at all.
        Quuen Elizabeth's reply.

> No mistress of the hidden skill,
>   No wizard gaunt and grim,
> Went up by night on heath or hill
>   To read the stars for him;
> But the merriest maid in all the land
>   Of vine-encircled France
> Bestowed upon his brow and hand
>   Her philsophic glance:
> "I bind thee with a spell," said she,
>   "I sign thee with a sign;
> No woman's love shall light on thee,
>   No woman's heart be thine!"
>   *Mrs. Hemans, The Child's Destiny.*

I remember, I remember,
   How my childhood fleeted by
The mirth of its December,
   And the warmth of its July.   *W. M. Praed.*

I love it, I love it, and who shall dare
To chide me for loving that old armchair?   *Eliza Cook.*

Oft in the stilly night,
Ere slumber's chain has bound me,
Fond memory brings the light
   Of others days around me!
   The smiles, the tears
      Of boyhood's years,
   The words of love then spoken;
   The eyes that shone,
      Now dimmed and gone,
      The cheerful hearts now broken!

   .   .   .   .

   I feel like one
   Who treads alone
Some banquet-hall deserted,
      Whose lights are fled,
      Whose garlands dead,
And all but he departed!   *Thomas Moore.*

The old oaken bucket, the iron-bound bucket,
The moss-covered bucket, which hung in the well.
                              Samuel Woodworth.

Near the lake where drooped the willow,
   Long time ago!   *George P. Morris.*

Woodman, spare that tree!
   Touch not a single bough!
In youth it sheltered me.
   And I'll protect it now.   *George P. Morris.*

   When the sun sinks to rest,
   And the star of the west
Sheds its soft silver light o'er the sea,
   What sweet thoughts arise,
   As the dim twilight dies—

For then I am thinking of thee,
  O ! then crowding fast
  Come the joys of the past,
Through the dimness of days long gone by,
  Like the stars peeping out.
  Through the darkness about,
From the soft silent depth of the sky.

  And thus, as the night
  Grows more lovely and bright
With the clustering of planet and star,
  So this darkness of mine
  Wins a radiance divine
From the light that still lingers afar.
  Then welcome the night,
  With its soft holy light!
In its silence my heart is more free
  The rude world to forget,
  Where no pleasure I've met
Since the hour that I parted from thee.   *Samuel Lover.*

Through days of sorrow and of mirth,
Through days of death and days of birth.
Through every swift vicissitude
Of changeful time, unchanged it has stood.
And as if, like God, it all things saw,
It calmly repeats those words of awe—
    "Forever—never!
    Never—forever!"   *Longfellow, The Old Clock.*

Stone walls do not a prison make,
  Nor iron bars a cage;
Minds innocent and quiet take
  That for an hermitage.   *Richard Lovelace.*

Could we forbear dispute and practice love.
We should agree as angels do above.   *Waller.*

I hold every man a debtor to his profession; from the
which as men of course do seek to receive countenance and
profit, so ought they of duty to endeavor themselves by way of
amends to be a help and ornament thereunto.   *Bacon.*

244

Music hath charms to soothe the savage breast,
To soften rocks, or bend a knotted oak, . . .
By magic numbers and persuasive sound.   *Congreve.*

When Music, heavenly maid, was young,
While yet in early Greece she sung.

.   .   .   .

Filled with fury, rapt, inspired,

.   .   .   .

'Twas sad by fits, by starts 'twas wild.

.   .   .

In notes by distance made more sweet,
In hollow murmurs died away.

.   .   .

O Music! sphere-descended maid,
Friend of pleasure, wisdom's aid.

William Collins.

Come forth unto the light of things,
    Let Nature be your teacher.

.   .   .   .

One impulse from a vernal wood
May teach you more of man,
Of moral evil and of good.
    Than all the sages can.   *Wordsworth.*

The melancholy days are come, the saddest of the year,
    Of wailing winds, and naked woods, and meadows brown
    and sere.
Heaped in the hollows of the grove the withered leaves
    lie dead.
They rustle to the eddying gust, and to the rabbit's tread.
                                            W. C. Bryant.

Nature, before it has been touched by man, is almost always beautiful, strong, and cheerful in man's eyes; but nature,
when he has once given it his culture and then forsakes it, has
usually an air of sorrow and helplessness. He has made it live
the more by laying his hand upon it, and touching it with his
life. It has come to relish of his humanity. and it is so flavored
with his thoughts, and ordered and permeated by his spirit, that
if the stimulus of his presence is withdrawn it cannot for a long

while do without him, and live for itself as fully and as well as
it did before.   *Jean Ingelow.*

>The sea! the sea! the open sea!
>The blue, the fresh, the ever free,
>Without a mark, without a bound,
>It runneth the earth's wide region round.
>
>.   .   .   .
>
>I never was on the dull, tame shore,
>But I loved the great sea more and more,
>And backward flew to her billowy breast,
>Like a bird that seeketh its mother's nest.
>
>   *Bryan W. Procter.*

>Like a spear of flame the cardinal flower
>Burned out along the meadow.   *Eddy.*

>A strong nor'wester's blowing, Bill;
>   Hark, don't ye hear it roar now!
>Lord help 'em, how I pities them
>   Unhappy folks on shore now!
>
>   *William Pitt.*

>Dearest, has Heaven aught to give thee more?
>   I thought the while I watched her changing face,
>   Heard her fine tones and marked her gestures' grace—
>Yea, one more gift is left all gifts before.
>
>We go our separate ways on earth, and pain,
>   God's shaping chisel, waits us as the rest,
>   With nobler charm thy beauty to invest,
>And make thee lovelier ere we meet again.
>
>   *Celia Thaxter.*

>Not perfect, nay, but full of tender wants
>No angel, but a dearer being, all dipt
>In angel instincts, breathing Paradise.   *Tennyson.*

Sink or swim, live or die, survive or perish, I give my heart
and my hand to this vote.   *Webster.*

The Guard dies, but never surrenders.   *Rougemont.*

There is one certain means by which I can be sure never
to see my country's ruin—*I will die in the last ditch.*

                            William of Orange.

Caesar had his Brutus—Charles the First, his Cromwell—
and George the Third ("Treason!" cried the Speaker)— *may
profit by their example.* If *this* be treason, make the most of it.
Patrick Henry.

Praise the Power that hath made and preserved us a na-
tion!
Then conquer we must, when our cause it is just,
And this be our motto: "In God is our trust;"
And the star-spangled banner, O long may it wave
O'er the land of the free, and the home of the brave.
Francis Scott Key.

Forever floats that standard sheet!
  Where breathes the foe but falls before us,
With Freedom's soil beneath our feet,
  And Freedom's banner streaming o'er us.
Joseph Rodman Drake.

Give me liberty or give me death!   *Patrick Henry.*

A song for our banner? The watchword recall
  Which gave the Republic her station:
"United we stand—divided we fall!"
  It made and preserves us a nation!
The union of lakes—the union of lands—
  The union of States none can sever—
The union of hearts, the union of hands—
  And the flag of our Union forever!   *George P. Morris.*

O rally 'round the flag, boys, rally once again,
  Shouting the battle-cry of Freedom.   *George F. Root.*

We join ourselves to no party that does not carry the flag
and keep step to the music of the Union.   *Rufus Choate.*

When can their glory fade?
Oh! the wild charge they made!
  All the world wondered.
Honour the charge they made!
Honour the Light Brigade,
  Noble six hundred!   *Tennyson.*

And he gave it as his opinion, that whoever could make
two ears of corn, or two blades of grass, to grow upon a spot

247

of ground where only one grew before, would deserve better of mankind, and do more esssential service to his country, than the whole race of politicians put together.

Swift, Gulliver's Travels.

I never could believe that Providence had sent a few men into the world ready booted and spurred to ride, and millions ready saddled and bridled to be ridden.

Richard Rumbold, on the scaffold.

Millions for defense, but not one cent for tribute.

C. C. Pinckney.

To the memory of the Man, first in war, first in peace, and first in the hearts of his countrymen. *General Henry Lee.*

But whether on the scaffold high,
　Or in the battle's van,
The fittest place where man can die
　Is where he dies for man. *Michael J. Barry.*

Let the soldier be abroad if he will, he can do nothing in this age. There is another personage, a personage less imposing in the eyes of some, perhaps insignificant. The schoolmaster is abroad, and I trust to him, armed with his primer, against the solder in full military array. *Lord Brougham.*

O for a seat in some poetic nook,
Just hid with trees, and sparkling with a brook.

Leigh Hunt.

In winter, when the dismal rain
　Came slanting down in lines,
And Wind, that grand old harper, smote
　His thunder-harp of pines. *Alexander Smith.*

There were two or three pretty faces among the female singers, to which the keen air of a frosty morning had given a bright rosy tint; but the gentlemen choristers had evidently been chosen, like old Cremona fiddles, more for tone than looks; and as several had to sing from the same book, there were clusterings of odd physiognomies, not unlike those groups of cherubs we sometimes see on country tombstones. *Irving.*

Seemed washing his hands with invisible soap
　In imperceptible water. *Hood.*

248

Reason is the life of the law; nay, the common law itself
is nothing else but reason. . . . The law which is the perfection of reason.   *Coke.*

Remorse—she ne'er forsakes us—
A bloodhound staunch—she tracks our rapid step
Through the wild labyrinth of youthful frenzy,
Unheard, perchance, until old age hath tamed us;
Then in our lair, when Time hath chilled our joints,
And maimed our hope of combat, or of flight,
We hear her deep-mouthed bay, announcing all
Of wrath, and woe, and punishment that bides us.

Old Play.

Do what lieth in thy power, and God will assist in thy
good will.   *Thomas à Kempis.*

Weep no more, lady, weep no more,
    Thy sorrow is in vaine;
For violets pluckt, the sweetest showers
    Will ne'er make grow againe.   *Thomas Percy.*

God will not give any soldier ammunition who is not willing to go into battle.   *Anon.*

What does little baby say,
In her bed at peep of day?
Baby says, like little birdie,
Let me rise and fly away.

Baby, sleep a little longer,
Till the little limbs are stronger.
If she sleeps a little longer
    Baby, too, shall fly away.

Tennyson.

Sweet and low, sweet and low,
    Wind of the western sea,
Low, low, breathe and blow,
    Wind of the western sea!
Over the rolling waters go,
Come from the dying moon and blow,
    Blow him again to me:
While my little one, while my pretty one, sleeps.

Sleep and rest, sleep and rest,
  Father will come to thee soon;
Rest, rest, on mother's breast,
  Father will come to thee soon;
Father will come to his babe in the nest,
Silver sails all out of the west,
  Under the silver moon:
Sleep, my little one, sleep, my pretty one, sleep.

Tennyson, The Princess.

Were I to adopt a pet idea as so many people do, and fondle it in my embraces to the exclusion of all others, it would be, that the great want which mankind labors under at this present period is sleep. The world should recline its vast head on the first convenient pillow and take an age-long nap. It has gone distracted through a morbid activity, and, while preternaturally wide awake, is nevertheless tormented by visions that seem real to it now, but would assume their true aspect and character were all things once set right by an interval of sound repose.

Hawthorne.

Oh! would I were dead now
Or up in my bed now,
To cover my head now,
  And have a good cry!   Thomas Hood.

When death, the great Reconciler, has come, it is never our tenderness that we repent of, but our severity.   George Eliot.

My best thoughts always come a little too late.

Hawthorne.

Thought is deeper than all speech;
  Feeling deeper than all thought;
Souls to souls can never teach
  What unto themselves was taught.

Christopher P. Cranch.

Too late I stayed—forgive the crime—
  Unheeded flew the hours;
How noiseless falls the foot of time,
  That only treads on flowers.   Wm. Robt. Spencer.

Gather ye rosebuds while ye may.
   Old Time is still a-flying,
And this same flower that smiles to-day,
   To-morrow may be dying.   *Robert Herrick.*

O! a wonderful stream is the river Time,
   As it runs through the realm of tears!
With a faultless rhythm, and a musical rhyme,
And a broader sweep and a surge sublime,
   As it blends in the oceans of years!   *B. F. Taylor.*

    By Woden, God of Saxons,
From whom comes Wensday, that, is, Wednesday.
Truth is a thing that I will ever keep
Unto thylke day in which I creep into
My sepulcre.   *Cartwright.*

O God, who art the truth, make me one with Thee in
everlasting love.   *Thomas à Kempis*